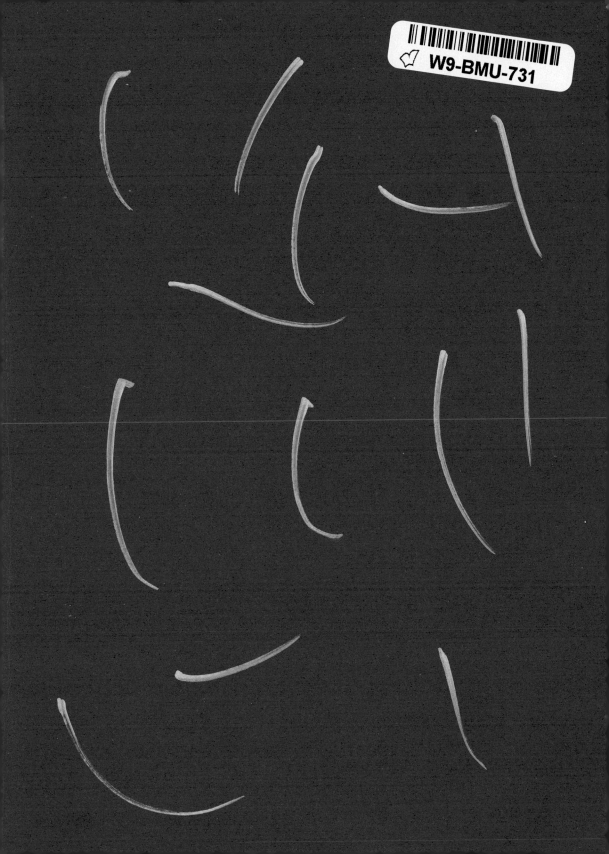

QUINOA
& OTHER GRAINS

pil

Publications International, Ltd.

Pictured on the front cover: Quinoa with Tomato, Broccoli and Feta *(page 150)*.
Pictured on the back cover *(top to bottom)*: Chicken Kabobs over Quinoa *(page 32)*, Quinoa-Stuffed Tomatoes *(page 128)*, and Orange Chicken Stir-Fry over Quinoa *(page 46)*.

ISBN-13: 978-1-68022-172-5

Library of Congress Control Number: 2015944922

Manufactured in China.

8 7 6 5 4 3 2 1

Microwave Cooking: Microwave ovens vary in wattage. Use the cooking times as guidelines and check for doneness before adding more time.

Preparation/Cooking Times: Preparation times are based on the approximate amount of time required to assemble the recipe before cooking, baking, chilling or serving. These times include preparation steps such as measuring, chopping and mixing. The fact that some preparations and cooking can be done simultaneously is taken into account. Preparation of optional ingredients and serving suggestions is not included.

Table of Contents

Breads & Breakfast

BERRY-QUINOA PARFAITS

Makes 6 servings

⅔ cup uncooked quinoa

2 cups plus 2 tablespoons
    fat-free (skim) milk, divided

⅛ teaspoon salt

¼ cup sugar

1 egg

1½ teaspoons vanilla

2 cups sliced strawberries

½ cup vanilla yogurt

Ground cinnamon (optional)

1. Place quinoa in fine-mesh strainer; rinse well under cold running water. Combine quinoa, 2 cups milk and salt in medium saucepan. Bring to a simmer over medium heat. Reduce heat to medium-low; simmer, uncovered, 20 to 25 minutes or until quinoa is tender, stirring frequently.

2. Whisk remaining 2 tablespoons milk, sugar, egg and vanilla in medium bowl until well blended. Gradually whisk ½ cup hot quinoa mixture into egg mixture, then whisk mixture back into saucepan. Cook over medium heat 3 to 5 minutes or until bubbly and thickened, stirring constantly. Remove from heat; let cool 30 minutes.

3. Layer quinoa mixture and strawberries in six parfait dishes. Top with dollop of yogurt and sprinkle with cinnamon, if desired.

BLUEBERRY PANCAKE SMILES

Makes about 16 small pancakes

½ **cup sorghum flour**

¼ **cup brown rice flour**

¼ **cup buckwheat flour***

2 **tablespoons sugar**

2 **teaspoons baking powder**

⅛ **teaspoon xanthan gum**

1 **to 1¼ cups rice milk**

**Equivalent 1 egg, prepared
powdered egg replacer**

2 **tablespoons vegetable oil**

1 **cup fresh blueberries**

Maple syrup (optional)

**Despite its name, there is no wheat or gluten in buckwheat. It's related to rhubarb.*

1. Combine sorghum flour, brown rice flour, buckwheat flour, sugar, baking powder and xanthan gum in medium bowl. Whisk in rice milk, egg replacer and oil until ingredients are moistened.

2. Spray large skillet with nonstick cooking spray. Heat over medium heat. Spoon batter into skillet 1 tablespoon at a time. Arrange blueberries on batter to make funny faces. Cook until bubbles cover surface of pancakes and bottoms are golden brown. Turn and cook 1 minute or until lightly browned. Serve, face side up, with maple syrup, if desired.

Tip: A delicious, fun and gluten-free recipe to share with your kids.

CRUNCHY WHOLE GRAIN BREAD

Makes 2 loaves

2 cups warm water (105°-115°F), divided

⅓ cup honey

2 tablespoons vegetable oil

1 tablespoon salt

2 packages (¼ ounce each) active dry yeast

2 to 2½ cups whole wheat flour, divided

1 cup bread flour

1¼ cups quick oats, divided

½ cup hulled pumpkin seeds or sunflower kernels

½ cup assorted grains and seeds

1 egg white

1 tablespoon water

1. Combine 1½ cups water, honey, oil and salt in small saucepan. Cook and stir over low heat until warm (115°-120°F).

2. Dissolve yeast in remaining ½ cup water in bowl of electric stand mixer. Let stand 5 minutes. Stir in honey mixture. Add 1 cup whole wheat flour and bread flour; knead with dough hook at low speed 2 minutes or until combined. Gradually stir in 1 cup oats, pumpkin seeds and assorted grains. Add remaining whole wheat flour, ½ cup at a time, just until dough begins to form a ball. Continue kneading 7 to 10 minutes or until dough is smooth and elastic.

3. Place dough in lightly oiled bowl, turning to coat top. Cover loosely with plastic wrap. Let rise in warm place 1½ to 2 hours or until doubled in bulk.

4. Grease two 9×5-inch loaf pans. Punch down dough. Divide in half. Shape each half into loaf; place in prepared pans. Cover with plastic wrap; let rise in warm place 1 hour or until almost doubled in bulk.

5. Preheat oven to 375°F. Whisk egg white and water in small bowl. Brush tops of loaves with egg mixture. Sprinkle with remaining ¼ cup oats. Bake 35 to 45 minutes or until loaves sound hollow when tapped. Cool loaves in pans 10 minutes. Remove to wire rack to cool completely.

Tip: This bread makes a delicious and healthy way to use up various grains and seeds you may have on hand.

BREAKFAST BITES

Makes 8 servings

½ cup mascarpone cheese

2 tablespoons packed brown sugar

2 tablespoons whipping cream

¼ teaspoon almond extract

⅔ cup whole wheat pastry flour

⅓ cup buckwheat flour

1 teaspoon baking powder

1 teaspoon stevia

1 teaspoon ground cinnamon

¼ teaspoon salt

2 eggs

¼ to ⅓ cup water

1 teaspoon vanilla

Fresh raspberries (optional)

1. For topping, combine mascarpone, brown sugar, whipping cream and almond extract in small bowl; set aside.

2. Mix pastry flour, buckwheat flour, baking powder, stevia, cinnamon and salt in medium bowl. Beat eggs, ¼ cup water and vanilla in another medium bowl until smooth. Whisk egg mixture into flour mixture, adding additional water 1 teaspoon at a time as needed, to make a thick batter.

3. Heat nonstick skillet or griddle. Drop about 2 tablespoons batter per pancake into skillet. Cook 2 to 3 minutes or until browned and puffy. Flip and cook another 2 to 3 minutes. Top each pancake with scant teaspoon of topping. Serve with fresh raspberries, if desired.

FRUIT-N-GRAIN BREAKFAST SALAD

Makes 6 servings

3 cups water

¼ teaspoon salt

¾ cup uncooked quick-cooking brown rice

¾ cup uncooked bulgur

1 Washington Granny Smith apple

1 Washington Red Delicious apple

1 orange

1 cup raisins

8 ounces lowfat vanilla yogurt

In large pot, bring water and salt to boil over high heat. Add rice and bulgur; reduce heat to low. Cover and cook 10 minutes. Remove from heat and set aside, covered, for 2 minutes. Spread hot grains on baking sheet to cool. (Grains can be cooked ahead of time and stored in refrigerator up to one week.) Just before serving, prepare fruit. Core and chop apples. Peel orange and cut into sections. Add chopped apple, orange sections and raisins to cooled grain mixture. Add yogurt and stir to coat grains and fruit.

courtesy of
Washington Apple Commission

QUINOA PANCAKES WITH TOMATO CHUTNEY

Makes 5 servings

Tomato Chutney

- 1 tablespoon vegetable oil
- ½ teaspoon cumin seeds
- ½ onion, finely chopped
- 2 cloves garlic, finely chopped
- 2 teaspoons grated fresh ginger
- 2 cups tomatoes, seeded and chopped
- 1 green chile, seeded and chopped (optional)
- 1 teaspoon ground coriander
- 1 teaspoon salt
- 2 teaspoons sugar

Pancakes

- 1 cup buttermilk pancake mix
- 1 cup red quinoa, cooked and cooled
- 1 egg, beaten
- 1¼ cups fat-free (skim) milk
- 1 cup spinach, finely chopped

1. To make chutney, heat oil in small skillet over medium heat. Add cumin seeds and cook a few seconds until seeds stop popping. Add onion, garlic and ginger. Cook 1 to 2 minutes until onion is translucent. Add tomatoes, green chile, coriander and salt. Cook 3 to 4 minutes until tomatoes are soft. Stir in sugar. Cool about 10 minutes.

2. Add chutney to blender. Blend slightly to reach uniform consistency, yet coarse texture. Serve immediately or cover and refrigerate. (It will keep in refrigerator up to 1 week.)

3. To make pancakes, combine pancake mix and quinoa in medium bowl. Mix in egg and milk. Fold in spinach. Let sit 10 minutes.

4. Spray medium skillet with nonstick cooking spray. Heat over medium heat. Pour ¼ cup batter onto heated skillet. Turn pancakes when top is bubbled and the bottom is light brown. Cook another 1 minute. Repeat with remaining batter. Serve warm with Tomato Chutney.

MIXED BERRY WHOLE GRAIN COFFEECAKE

Makes 12 servings

1¼ cups all-purpose flour, divided

¾ cup quick oats

¾ cup packed light brown sugar

3 tablespoons butter, softened

1 cup whole wheat flour

1 cup fat-free (skim) milk

¾ cup granulated sugar

¼ cup canola oil

1 egg, slightly beaten

1 tablespoon baking powder

1 teaspoon ground cinnamon

½ teaspoon salt

1½ cups frozen unsweetened mixed berries, thawed and drained *or* 2 cups fresh berries

¼ cup chopped walnuts

1. Preheat oven to 350°F. Spray 9×5-inch loaf pan with nonstick cooking spray.

2. Combine ¼ cup all-purpose flour, oats, brown sugar and butter in small bowl; mix with fork until crumbly.

3. Combine remaining 1 cup all-purpose flour, whole wheat flour, milk, granulated sugar, oil, egg, baking powder, cinnamon and salt in large bowl. Beat with electric mixer or whisk 1 to 2 minutes until well blended. Fold in berries. Spread batter in prepared pan; sprinkle evenly with oat mixture and walnuts.

4. Bake 38 to 40 minutes or until toothpick inserted into center comes out clean. Serve warm.

SUPER OATMEAL

Makes 5 to 6 servings

2 cups water

2¾ cups old-fashioned oats

½ cup finely diced dried figs*

⅓ cup lightly packed dark
   brown sugar

⅓ to ½ cup sliced almonds,
   toasted**

¼ cup flaxseeds

½ teaspoon salt

½ teaspoon ground cinnamon

2 cups reduced-fat (2%) or
   whole milk, plus additional
   for serving

*Beige Turkish figs are preferred if your market
carries them.*

**To toast almonds, spread in single layer on
baking sheet. Bake in preheated 350°F oven 8 to
10 minutes or until golden brown, stirring
frequently.*

1. Bring water to a boil over high heat in large saucepan. Stir in oats, figs, brown sugar, almonds, flaxseeds, salt and cinnamon. Immediately add 2 cups milk. Stir well.

2. Reduce heat to medium-high. Cook and stir 5 to 7 minutes or until oatmeal is thick and creamy. Spoon into individual bowls. Serve with additional milk, if desired.

BREAKFAST QUINOA

Makes 2 servings

½ **cup uncooked quinoa**

1 **cup water**

1 **tablespoon packed brown sugar**

2 **teaspoons maple syrup**

½ **teaspoon ground cinnamon**

¼ **cup golden raisins (optional)**

  Milk (optional)

  Fresh raspberries and banana slices

1. Place quinoa in fine-mesh strainer; rinse well under cold running water. Transfer to small saucepan.

2. Stir in water, brown sugar, maple syrup and cinnamon; bring to a boil over high heat. Reduce heat to low; cover and simmer 10 to 15 minutes or until quinoa is tender and water is absorbed. Add raisins, if desired, during last 5 minutes of cooking. Serve with milk, if desired; top with raspberries and bananas.

BUCKWHEAT PANCAKES

Makes 4 servings

1 cup buckwheat flour

2 tablespoons cornstarch

2 teaspoons baking powder

¼ teaspoon salt

¼ teaspoon ground cinnamon

1 cup whole milk

1 egg

2 tablespoons butter, melted,
    plus additional for cooking

2 tablespoons maple syrup, plus
    additional for serving

½ teaspoon vanilla

1. Whisk buckwheat flour, cornstarch, baking powder, salt and cinnamon in medium bowl. Whisk milk, egg, 2 tablespoons butter, 2 tablespoons maple syrup and vanilla in small bowl. Gradually whisk into dry ingredients just until combined. Let stand 5 minutes. (Batter will be thick and elastic.)

2. Brush additional butter on griddle or large nonstick skillet; heat over medium heat. Pour ¼ cupfuls of batter 2 inches apart onto griddle. Cook 2 minutes or until lightly browned and edges begin to bubble. Turn over; cook 2 minutes or until lightly browned. Serve with additional maple syrup.

Variation: Add ½ cup blueberries to the batter.

WHOLE GRAIN APRICOT SCONES

Makes 12 scones

1 cup *plus* 2 tablespoons
old-fashioned oats

1 cup whole-wheat flour

1 cup all-purpose flour

½ cup *dry* NESTLÉ®
CARNATION® Instant
Nonfat Dry Milk

½ cup packed brown sugar

2 teaspoons baking powder

⅔ cup butter, cut into pieces,
softened

1 cup (6-ounce package) dried
apricots, chopped

3 large eggs, *divided*

1 tablespoon water

PREHEAT oven to 425°F. Lightly grease baking sheet.

COMBINE *1 cup* oats, whole-wheat flour, all-purpose flour, dry milk, brown sugar and baking powder in large bowl. Cut in butter with pastry blender or two knives until mixture resembles coarse crumbs. Stir in apricots. Stir in *2 eggs,* just until blended. Do not over mix.

KNEAD dough 8 to 10 times on lightly floured surface. Pat into 9-inch circle and place on prepared baking sheet. Score top into 12 wedges with knife. Combine *remaining egg* and water in small bowl. Brush egg mixture over top of dough; sprinkle *remaining 2 tablespoons* oats over dough.

BAKE for 18 to 20 minutes or until edges are golden and wooden pick inserted in center comes out clean. Cool on baking sheet on wire rack for 10 minutes. Break or cut scones apart at scored lines. Serve warm. Store any remaining tightly covered.

Variation: 1 cup golden raisins, dried cranberries, dried blueberries or ½ cup currants can be substituted for the apricots.

Prep Time: 15 minutes

Baking Time: 20 minutes

ONION BUCKWHEAT BREAD

Makes 2 (10-inch) round loaves

1 pound diced white onions

3 tablespoons olive oil

4½ teaspoons yeast

1½ cups water, at 90°F

½ cup milk

6½ cups unbleached bread flour

½ cup buckwheat flour

5 teaspoons sea salt

1 tablespoon finely chopped
  fresh rosemary

¾ cup (3 ounces) shredded
  Gouda or Cheddar cheese

Unbleached bread flour as
  needed for kneading

4 tablespoons poppy seeds or
  nigella seeds (onion seeds)

1. Sauté onions in olive oil in large skillet over medium-high heat until just browned, about 5 minutes. Set aside to cool.

2. Combine yeast with water in large bowl; let sit 10 minutes until bubbly.

3. Add milk to yeast mixture; stir to combine.

4. Gradually add bread flour, buckwheat flour, salt, rosemary and onions to yeast mixture.

5. When mixture is well combined, add cheese and blend. The dough will be slightly sticky.

6. Knead dough on lightly floured surface about 10 minutes until smooth and elastic. Add additional bread flour as needed if dough is too soft.

7. Lightly oil clean bowl. Place dough in bowl; cover and let rise until doubled in bulk, 1½ to 2 hours.

8. Gently punch down dough and place on lightly floured surface. Cut dough in half and shape into round loaves. Spritz top of each loaf with water and press on poppy seeds or nigella seeds. Place on lightly floured baking sheet; cover and let rise until almost doubled in bulk, 45 minutes to 1 hour.

9. Preheat oven to 450°F. Slash tops of loaves with sharp knife and place in oven. Add steam by placing 2 ice cubes in pan on bottom of oven. Bake 10 minutes. *Reduce heat to 400°F* and bake an additional 35 to 40 minutes. Cool loaves completely on rack.

courtesy of National Onion Association

HONEY FIG WHOLE WHEAT MUFFINS

Makes 12 muffins

1 cup whole wheat flour

½ cup all-purpose flour

½ cup wheat germ

2 teaspoons baking powder

1 teaspoon ground cinnamon

½ teaspoon salt

½ teaspoon ground nutmeg

½ cup milk

½ cup honey

¼ cup (½ stick) butter, melted

1 egg

1 cup chopped dried figs

½ cup chopped walnuts

1. Preheat oven to 375°F. Grease 12 standard (2½-inch) muffin cups or line with paper baking cups.

2. Combine flours, wheat germ, baking powder, cinnamon, salt and nutmeg in large bowl. Combine milk, honey, butter and egg in small bowl until well blended. Stir into flour mixture just until moistened. Fold in figs and walnuts. Spoon evenly into prepared muffin cups.

3. Bake 20 minutes or until lightly browned on edges and toothpick inserted in center comes out clean. Remove from pan.

Hearty Dinners

SHRIMP, SNOW PEA AND QUINOA TOSS

Makes 4 servings

- ½ **cup uncooked quinoa**
- 1 **cup water**
- 8 **ounces large cooked shrimp, peeled and deveined with tails on**
- 8 **ounces (about 2½ cups) snow peas, steamed and cut in half, if large**
- 1 **teaspoon minced fresh dill, plus additional for garnish**
- 2 **tablespoons minced fresh chives**
- 3 **tablespoons orange juice**
- 1 **teaspoon lemon juice**
- 1 **tablespoon white wine vinegar**
- 2 **teaspoons olive oil**
- ½ **teaspoon salt**
- ¼ **teaspoon black pepper**

1. Place quinoa in fine-mesh strainer; rinse well under cold running water. Bring 1 cup water to a boil in small saucepan; stir in quinoa. Reduce heat to low; cover and simmer 15 minutes or until quinoa is tender and water is absorbed. Fluff with fork and set aside to cool.

2. Fluff quinoa again and place in serving bowl. Add shrimp, snow peas, 1 teaspoon dill and chives. Toss gently, but well.

3. Combine orange juice, lemon juice, vinegar, oil, salt and pepper in small cup. Pour over salad. Toss gently, but well. Garnish with additional dill.

CHICKEN KABOBS OVER QUINOA

Makes 4 servings

½ cup uncooked quinoa

1 cup water

1 jalapeño pepper,* seeded and finely chopped (optional)

3 teaspoons grated lemon peel, divided

½ teaspoon salt, divided

1 pound skinless boneless chicken breasts, cut into 16 (1-inch) cubes

2 teaspoons chicken seasoning blend

8 asparagus spears, trimmed and sliced into thirds

16 grape tomatoes

16 green onions, trimmed and folded in half

2 tablespoons lemon juice

2 tablespoons extra virgin olive oil

1 clove garlic, minced

¼ cup chopped fresh cilantro

Jalapeño peppers can sting and irritate the skin, so wear rubber gloves when handling peppers and do not touch your eyes.

1. Place quinoa in fine-mesh strainer; rinse well under cold running water. Bring 1 cup water to a boil in small saucepan; stir in quinoa. Reduce heat to low; cover and simmer 10 to 15 minutes or until quinoa is tender and water is absorbed. Remove from heat. Stir in jalapeño pepper, if desired, 2 teaspoons lemon peel and ¼ teaspoon salt. Keep warm.

2. Meanwhile, soak eight 12-inch wooden skewers in cold water 10 minutes. Sprinkle chicken cubes with seasoning blend. Thread chicken, asparagus, tomatoes and green onions onto skewers.

3. Combine lemon juice, remaining 1 teaspoon lemon peel, oil, garlic and remaining ¼ teaspoon salt in small bowl. Reserve half of mixture; brush remaining mixture over skewers.

4. Oil grid. Prepare grill for direct cooking. Grill skewers 3 to 4 minutes on each side or until chicken is cooked through.

5. Brush skewers with reserved lemon juice mixture. Stir cilantro into quinoa; serve with chicken and vegetable kabobs.

QUINOA, TURKEY AND APPLE PILAF

Makes 4 servings

½ **cup uncooked quinoa**

1 **cup water**

1 **tablespoon canola oil**

1½ **cups chopped onions**

1 **cup chopped red bell pepper**

1 **cup diced red apple**

6 **ounces cooked oven-roasted turkey breast, chopped**

2 **ounces pecan pieces, toasted**

⅓ **cup dried apricot halves, chopped**

¼ **cup chopped fresh cilantro (optional)**

1 to 1½ **teaspoons grated fresh ginger**

1½ **teaspoons sugar**

½ **teaspoon salt**

1. Place quinoa in fine-mesh strainer; rinse well under cold running water. Bring 1 cup water to a boil in small saucepan; stir in quinoa. Reduce heat to low; cover and simmer 15 minutes or until quinoa is tender and water is absorbed. Fluff with fork and set aside to cool.

2. Meanwhile, heat oil in large nonstick skillet over medium-high heat. Cook onions 5 minutes or until beginning to richly brown. Stir in bell pepper and apple; cook 4 minutes or until apple is just crisp-tender. Add turkey and cook 1 minute. Remove from heat, stir in quinoa and remaining ingredients. Cover and let stand 5 minutes to absorb flavors.

SAUSAGE AND SQUASH RAFTS

Makes 4 servings

⅓ **cup uncooked bulgur wheat**

1 small onion, finely chopped

1 clove garlic, minced

2 raw sweet Italian turkey sausage links (about 3 ounces each), casings removed

¼ **teaspoon ground cumin**

⅛ **teaspoon black pepper**

2 tablespoons finely chopped dried cranberries

1 (2-pound) butternut squash

¾ **cup chicken broth**

2 tablespoons chopped fresh parsley (optional)

1. Preheat oven to 400°F. Place bulgur in heatproof bowl. Cover with boiling water; set aside 30 minutes. Meanwhile, spray large skillet with nonstick cooking spray. Add onion and garlic; cook over medium heat 5 minutes, stirring frequently. Drain bulgur in wire mesh stainer.

2. Brown sausage in skillet, stirring to break up meat. Stir in cumin, pepper and cranberries. Stir bulgur into sausage mixture.

3. Place squash on its side. Using a very sharp knife, cut 4 slices crosswise about 1 inch thick. Remove and discard seeds. Pour broth into shallow roasting pan. Arrange slices, cavity-side up, in pan.

4. Roast squash 30 to 35 minutes or until almost tender. Remove from oven, turn slices over. Spoon about ½ cup sausage mixture on each squash slice. Baste sausage mixture with broth. Bake 10 minutes or until squash is tender. Garnish with chopped parsley.

QUICK BARLEY WITH CHICKEN, PEAS AND CARROTS

Makes 4 servings

1 cup diced carrots

½ cup diced celery

½ cup diced onion

1 can (about 14 ounces) chicken broth

⅔ cup uncooked quick-cooking barley

½ cup water

½ teaspoon salt

⅛ teaspoon black pepper

2 cups diced cooked boneless skinless chicken breast

1 cup frozen peas, thawed

⅓ cup chopped fresh Italian parsley

1. Spray large skillet with nonstick cooking spray; heat over medium-high heat. Add carrots, celery and onion; cook and stir 6 minutes or until browned in spots.

2. Stir in broth, barley, water, salt and pepper. Cover and bring to a boil. Reduce heat to medium-low; simmer 12 minutes or until barley is tender. Stir in chicken, peas and parsley. Remove from heat. Cover and let stand 5 minutes.

ROASTED SALMON AND ASPARAGUS WITH QUINOA

Makes 4 servings

1 pound fresh thin asparagus spears

2½ teaspoons olive oil, divided

8 ounces wild-caught salmon fillet

½ teaspoon salt, divided

¼ teaspoon black pepper, divided

½ cup uncooked quinoa

1 cup water

1 green onion, chopped

1 teaspoon lemon juice

½ teaspoon minced fresh dill

4 lemon wedges (optional)

1. Preheat oven to 400°F. Snap tough ends off asparagus. Place in large nonstick roasting pan. Drizzle with 1 teaspoon oil. Roast 10 minutes. Turn asparagus and push to one side of pan. Arrange salmon, skin side down, on other side. Brush with ½ teaspoon oil, sprinkle with ¼ teaspoon salt and ⅛ teaspoon pepper. Roast 10 to 13 minutes or until salmon is cooked through. Remove asparagus and cut into bite-size pieces. Remove skin from salmon.

2. Meanwhile, place quinoa in fine-mesh strainer; rinse well under cold running water. Bring 1 cup water to a boil in small saucepan; stir in quinoa. Reduce heat to low; cover and simmer 10 to 15 minutes or until quinoa is tender and water is absorbed. Transfer to large bowl.

3. Stir in asparagus, green onion, remaining 1 teaspoon oil, ¼ teaspoon salt, ⅛ teaspoon pepper, lemon juice and dill. Transfer to 4 plates; top with salmon. Garnish with lemon wedges, if desired.

SWEET CURRIED CHICKEN AND QUINOA SALAD

Makes 2 servings

⅓ cup uncooked quinoa

1 cup water

2 tablespoons sliced almonds

1 boneless skinless chicken breast (4 ounces), cut into ½-inch cubes

1 tablespoon plus 1½ teaspoons mayonnaise

1 tablespoon plus 1½ teaspoons sour cream

1½ teaspoons sugar substitute*

1 teaspoon curry powder

¼ teaspoon ground cumin

⅛ teaspoon salt

½ cup very thinly sliced celery

¼ cup finely chopped red onion

3 tablespoons golden raisins or regular raisins

4 baby spinach leaves

*This recipe was tested using sucralose-based sugar substitute.

1. Place quinoa in fine-mesh strainer; rinse well under cold running water. Bring 1 cup water to a boil in small saucepan over high heat. Stir in quinoa; reduce heat to medium-low. Cover and simmer 15 to 18 minutes or until liquid is absorbed and quinoa is tender. Let cool.

2. Heat large nonstick skillet over medium-high heat. Add almonds; cook and stir 3 to 4 minutes or until lightly browned. Set aside on plate. Spray skillet with nonstick cooking spray. Cook and stir chicken 3 to 5 minutes or until cooked through. Let cool.

3. Combine mayonnaise, sour cream, sugar substitute, curry powder, cumin and salt in medium bowl. Stir until well blended. Stir in celery, onion and raisins.

4. Add chicken, almonds and quinoa; stir gently until blended. Let stand 10 minutes to blend flavors. Serve over spinach leaves.

BARLEY BEEF STROGANOFF

Makes 4 servings

2½ **cups vegetable broth or water**

⅔ **cup uncooked pearl barley (not quick-cooking)**

1 **package (6 ounces) sliced mushrooms**

½ **teaspoon dried marjoram**

½ **teaspoon black pepper**

½ **pound ground beef**

½ **cup chopped celery**

½ **cup minced green onions**

¼ **cup half-and-half**

Minced fresh parsley (optional)

Slow Cooker Directions

1. Place broth, barley, mushrooms, marjoram and pepper in slow cooker. Cover; cook on LOW 6 to 7 hours.

2. Brown beef in large skillet over medium-high heat 6 to 8 minutes, stirring to break up meat. Drain fat. Add celery and green onions; cook and stir 3 minutes.

3. Turn slow cooker to HIGH. Stir beef mixture and half-and-half into slow cooker mixture. Cover; cook on HIGH 10 to 15 minutes or until beef is hot and vegetables are tender. Garnish with parsley.

ORANGE CHICKEN STIR-FRY OVER QUINOA

Makes 4 servings

- ½ **cup uncooked quinoa**
- 1 **cup water**
- 2 **teaspoons vegetable oil, divided**
- 1 **pound boneless skinless chicken breasts, cut into thin strips**
- 1 **cup fresh squeezed orange juice (2 to 3 oranges)**
- 1 **tablespoon soy sauce**
- 1 **tablespoon cornstarch**
- ½ **cup sliced green onions**
- 2 **tablespoons grated fresh ginger**
- 6 **ounces snow peas, ends trimmed**
- 1 **cup thinly sliced carrots**
- ¼ **teaspoon red pepper flakes (optional)**

1. Place quinoa in fine-mesh strainer; rinse well under cold running water. Bring 1 cup water to a boil in medium saucepan; stir in quinoa. Reduce heat to low; cover and simmer 10 to 15 minutes or until quinoa is tender and water is absorbed.

2. Meanwhile, heat 1 teaspoon oil in large skillet over medium-high heat. Add chicken; cook and stir 4 to 6 minutes or until no longer pink. Remove to plate; keep warm.

3. Stir orange juice and soy sauce into cornstarch in small bowl until smooth; set aside. Heat remaining 1 teaspoon oil in skillet. Add green onions and ginger; stir-fry 1 to 2 minutes. Add snow peas and carrots; stir-fry 4 to 5 minutes or until carrots are crisp-tender.

4. Return chicken to skillet. Stir orange juice mixture; add to skillet. Bring to a boil. Reduce heat; simmer until slightly thickened.

5. Serve chicken and vegetables over quinoa; sprinkle with red pepper flakes, if desired.

CRUNCHY QUINOA FISH STICKS WITH EASY TARTAR SAUCE

Makes 4 servings

Easy Tartar Sauce (recipe follows)

2 teaspoons butter

¾ cup panko bread crumbs

¼ cup uncooked quinoa

1 teaspoon smoked paprika

½ teaspoon salt

¼ cup whole wheat flour

2 egg whites, lightly beaten

¾ pound wild Alaskan cod, cut into ½-inch-wide strips

Lemon wedges (optional)

1. Preheat oven to 425°F. Line baking sheet with parchment paper. Prepare Easy Tartar Sauce.

2. Melt butter in small skillet over medium heat. Add panko, quinoa, paprika and salt; cook and stir 5 minutes or until golden brown. Remove to shallow bowl. Place flour in another shallow bowl. Place egg whites in separate shallow bowl.

3. Working one at a time, coat fish with flour; shake off excess. Dip in egg whites, letting excess drip back into bowl. Roll in panko mixture, pressing lightly to adhere. Place on prepared baking sheet. Repeat with remaining fish.

4. Bake 12 minutes or until fish is opaque in center and flakes easily when tested with fork. Serve with Easy Tartar Sauce. Garnish with lemon wedges.

Easy Tartar Sauce: Combine ½ cup low-fat mayonnaise, ¼ cup sweet pickle relish and 2 teaspoons lemon juice in small bowl; mix well. Refrigerate until ready to serve. Makes about ½ cup.

SOUTH AMERICAN CHICKEN AND QUINOA

Makes 4 servings

**Tomato-Apricot Chutney
(recipe follows)**

1 teaspoon ground turmeric

1 teaspoon dried thyme

¾ teaspoon salt, divided

1 pound boneless skinless
chicken breasts, cut into
1-inch pieces

2 tablespoons olive oil, divided

1 large red or green bell pepper,
chopped

1 medium onion, chopped

1 cup uncooked quinoa

1 cup chicken broth

1 cup unsweetened coconut
milk

1 teaspoon curry powder

¼ teaspoon ground ginger

1. Prepare Tomato-Apricot Chutney; set aside.

2. Combine turmeric, thyme and ¼ teaspoon salt in shallow dish. Coat chicken pieces with spice mixture; set aside.

3. Heat 1 tablespoon oil in large skillet over medium-high heat. Add bell pepper and onion; cook and stir 2 minutes or until vegetables are crisp-tender. Remove from skillet; set aside.

4. Add remaining 1 tablespoon oil to skillet. Add chicken pieces; cook and stir 5 minutes or until golden brown and cooked through.

5. Place quinoa in fine-mesh strainer; rinse well under cold running water. Combine quinoa, broth, coconut milk, curry powder, remaining ½ teaspoon salt and ginger in large saucepan. Bring to a boil over high heat. Reduce heat to low; cover and simmer 10 minutes.

6. Stir chicken and pepper mixture into quinoa; cook 5 minutes or until liquid is absorbed and quinoa is tender. Serve with Tomato-Apricot Chutney.

TOMATO-APRICOT CHUTNEY

¾ **cup apple cider or apple juice**

¾ **cup finely diced dried apricots**

½ **cup currants or golden raisins**

3 to 4 tablespoons cider vinegar

1 can (about 14 ounces) diced tomatoes, drained

1 tablespoon packed dark brown sugar

1 teaspoon ground ginger

⅛ **teaspoon ground cloves**

1. Combine apple cider, apricots, currants and vinegar in small saucepan. Bring to a boil over high heat. Reduce heat to low; cover and simmer 10 minutes.

2. Stir in tomatoes, brown sugar, ginger and cloves; simmer, uncovered, 5 minutes or until liquid is absorbed.

CHICKEN WITH CURRIED BULGUR

Makes 4 servings

1¼ **cups water, divided**

½ **teaspoon salt, divided**

½ **cup uncooked bulgur wheat**

4 **boneless skinless chicken breasts (about 1 pound)**

½ **teaspoon ground cumin, divided**

¼ **teaspoon black pepper**

½ **cup raisins**

¼ **cup slivered almonds, toasted***

¼ **cup chopped green onions, divided**

½ **teaspoon curry powder**

½ **teaspoon grated fresh ginger**

*To toast almonds, spread in shallow baking pan. Bake in preheated 350°F oven 5 to 7 minutes or until fragrant, stirring occasionally.

1. Bring 1 cup water and ¼ teaspoon salt to a boil in small saucepan over high heat; stir in bulgur. Cover; remove from heat and let stand 10 minutes or until liquid is absorbed and bulgur is tender.

2. Meanwhile, sprinkle chicken with remaining ¼ teaspoon salt, ¼ teaspoon cumin and pepper. Spray large skillet with nonstick cooking spray; heat over medium-high heat. Cook chicken 4 to 5 minutes on each side or until no longer pink in center. Remove from skillet; keep warm.

3. Combine remaining ¼ cup water, raisins, almonds, 2 tablespoons green onions, curry powder, ginger and remaining ¼ teaspoon cumin in skillet. Bring to a boil. Reduce heat; fluff bulgur and add to skillet, tossing until combined.

4. Serve chicken on bulgur mixture; sprinkle with remaining 2 tablespoons green onions.

BEEF FILETS WITH ANCIENT GRAIN & KALE SALAD

Makes 2 servings

2 beef Tenderloin Steaks, cut 1 inch thick (about 6 ounces each)

3 cloves garlic, minced, divided

¼ plus ⅛ teaspoon cracked black pepper, divided

1 cup reduced-sodium beef broth

½ cup pearlized farro

1 cup thinly sliced kale

¼ cup dried sweetened cranberries or cherries

2 tablespoons sliced almonds

2 teaspoons fresh lemon juice

Salt

1. Combine 1 clove garlic and ¼ teaspoon pepper; press evenly onto beef steaks.

2. Combine beef broth, farro, remaining 2 cloves garlic and remaining ⅛ teaspoon pepper in small saucepan. Bring to a boil; reduce heat to low. Cover and simmer 15 to 20 minutes or until most broth has been absorbed. Remove from heat. Stir in kale and cranberries. Cover; let stand 5 minutes. Stir in almonds and lemon juice. Season with salt, as desired.

3. Meanwhile, place steaks on rack in broiler pan so surface of steaks is 2 to 3 inches from heat. Broil 13 to 16 minutes for medium rare (145°F) to medium (160°F) doneness, turning once.

4. Season steaks with salt. Serve with farro mixture.

Cook's Tip: Quick (pearled) barley or long-grain brown rice may be substituted for farro. Cook according to package directions using ½ cup preferred grain and 1 cup reduced-sodium beef broth. Stir in kale and cranberries. Cover; let stand 5 minutes. Stir in almonds and lemon juice. Season with salt, as desired.

courtesy of The Beef Checkoff

CHICKEN WITH PEAS & QUINOA

Makes 4 servings

1 tablespoon olive oil

1 pound skinless, boneless
    chicken tenders

1 teaspoon smoked paprika

1 cup *uncooked* quinoa, rinsed

1½ cups SWANSON® Chicken
    Broth *or* SWANSON®
    Chicken Stock

1 jar (24 ounces) PREGO®
    VEGGIE SMART® Smooth
    & Simple Italian Sauce

1 package (10 ounces) frozen
    peas, thawed

1. Heat the oil in a 12-inch skillet over medium-high heat. Add the chicken and cook for 10 minutes or until well browned on both sides. Remove the chicken from the skillet, cover and keep warm.

2. Add the paprika and quinoa to the skillet and stir to coat. Stir in the broth and Italian sauce and heat to a boil. Reduce the heat to medium. Cover and cook for 15 minutes or until the quinoa is tender. Stir in the peas. Return the chicken to the skillet. Cook until the chicken is cooked through.

Prep Time: 10 minutes
Cook Time: 30 minutes

SALMON IN THE WILD

Makes 4 servings

1 package (6 ounces) long grain and wild rice

1 tablespoon butter or margarine, cut into small pieces

½ cup shredded carrot

2 cups boiling water

1 pound salmon fillets, skin removed

⅓ cup teriyaki sauce

1 sliced orange (optional)

1. Preheat oven to 350°F. Pour rice and contents of seasoning packet into 8-inch square baking dish. Dot top of rice with butter and top with carrot. Pour boiling water into baking dish.

2. Cut salmon into 8 pieces and evenly space on top of rice mixture. Cover dish with foil and bake 20 minutes. Remove foil; bake 5 minutes longer.

3. Spoon rice and salmon onto serving plates; drizzle salmon with teriyaki sauce. Garnish with orange slices.

TURKEY MEAT LOAF

Makes 5 servings

1 tablespoon vegetable oil

¾ cup chopped onion

½ cup chopped celery

1 clove garlic, minced

⅔ cup chicken broth or water

½ cup uncooked bulgur wheat

½ cup cholesterol-free egg substitute

1 tablespoon soy sauce

¼ teaspoon ground cumin

¼ teaspoon paprika

¼ teaspoon black pepper

1 pound ground turkey

8 tablespoons chili sauce, divided

1. Heat oil in medium skillet over medium heat. Add onion, celery and garlic; cook and stir 3 minutes. Add broth and bulgur. Bring to a boil. Reduce heat to low; cover and simmer 10 to 15 minutes or until bulgur is tender and all liquid is absorbed. Transfer to large bowl; cool to lukewarm.

2. Preheat oven to 375°F. Stir egg substitute, soy sauce, cumin, paprika and pepper into bulgur. Add ground turkey and 6 tablespoons chili sauce. Stir until well blended.

3. Pat turkey mixture into greased 8½×4½-inch loaf pan. Top with remaining 2 tablespoons chili sauce.

4. Bake meat loaf about 45 minutes or until internal temperature reaches 165°F. Let stand 10 minutes. Remove from pan; cut into 10 slices.

TURKEY SANDWICHES WITH ROASTED BELL PEPPERS

Makes 4 servings

2 large red bell peppers

8 slices whole grain *or* millet bread

¼ cup mayonnaise

8 spinach leaves *or* 4 romaine lettuce leaves

8 thin slices red onion

½ pound thinly sliced skinless roasted turkey breast

8 large fresh basil leaves (optional)

1. Preheat broiler. Cut bell peppers into quarters; discard stems, membranes and seeds. Place peppers, skin side up, on foil-lined baking sheet. Broil 3 inches from heat 10 minutes or until skin is blackened. Wrap peppers in foil from baking sheet; let stand 10 minutes. Peel off skin and discard.

2. Spread 4 bread slices with mayonnaise. Top with spinach, onion, turkey, peppers and basil, if desired. Top with remaining bread slices.

SPROUTS AND BULGUR SANDWICHES

Makes 4 servings

½ **cup bulgur wheat**

1 **cup water**

1 **container (8 ounces) plain
low-fat yogurt**

¼ **cup salad dressing or
mayonnaise**

1½ **teaspoons curry powder**

1 **cup shredded carrots**

½ **cup chopped apple**

⅓ **cup coarsely chopped peanuts**

2 **cups fresh bean sprouts**

8 **very thin slices wheat bread,
toasted**

1. Rinse bulgur under cold running water; drain. Bring 1 cup water to a boil in small saucepan over high heat. Stir in bulgur. Remove from heat. Let stand, uncovered, 20 minutes. Drain well; squeeze out excess liquid.

2. Combine yogurt, salad dressing and curry powder in medium bowl. Stir in bulgur, carrots, apple and peanuts. Cover and refrigerate.

3. Arrange sprouts on 4 slices wheat toast. Spread with bulgur mixture. Top with remaining bread slices.

ASIAN PESTO NOODLES

Makes 4 servings

Spicy Asian Pesto (recipe follows)

1 pound large raw shrimp, peeled and deveined

12 ounces uncooked soba (buckwheat) noodles

1. Prepare Spicy Asian Pesto. Marinate shrimp in ¾ cup pesto.

2. Cook soba noodles according to package directions; drain and set aside. Preheat broiler or grill.

3. Place marinated shrimp on metal skewers. (If using wooden skewers, soak in water for at least 30 minutes to prevent burning.) Place skewers under broiler or on grill; cook about 3 minutes per side or until shrimp are opaque.

4. To serve, toss soba noodles with remaining pesto. Serve with shrimp.

SPICY ASIAN PESTO

Makes 2½ cups

3 cups fresh basil

3 cups fresh cilantro

3 cups fresh mint

¾ cup peanut oil

3 tablespoons sugar

2 to 3 tablespoons lime juice

5 cloves garlic, chopped

2 teaspoons fish sauce *or* 1 teaspoon salt

1 serrano pepper,* finely chopped

Combine all ingredients in blender or food processor; blend until smooth.

*Serrano peppers can sting and irritate the skin, so wear rubber gloves when handling peppers and do not touch your eyes.

Meatless Meals

QUINOA BURRITO BOWLS

Makes 4 servings

1 cup uncooked quinoa

2 cups water

2 tablespoons fresh lime juice, divided

¼ cup sour cream

2 teaspoons vegetable oil

1 small onion, diced

1 red bell pepper, diced

1 clove garlic, minced

½ cup canned black beans, rinsed and drained

½ cup thawed frozen corn

Shredded lettuce

Lime wedges (optional)

1. Place quinoa in fine-mesh strainer; rinse well under cold running water. Bring 2 cups water to a boil in small saucepan; stir in quinoa. Reduce heat to low; cover and simmer 10 to 15 minutes or until quinoa is tender and water is absorbed. Stir in 1 tablespoon lime juice. Cover and keep warm. Combine sour cream and remaining 1 tablespoon lime juice; set aside.

2. Meanwhile, heat oil in large skillet over medium heat. Add onion and bell pepper; cook and stir 5 minutes or until softened. Add garlic; cook 1 minute. Add black beans and corn; cook 3 to 5 minutes or until heated through.

3. Divide quinoa among 4 serving bowls; top with black bean mixture, lettuce and sour cream mixture. Garnish with lime wedges.

TABBOULEH IN TOMATO CUPS

Makes 4 servings

**4 large firm ripe tomatoes
  (about 8 ounces each)**

2 tablespoons olive oil

**4 green onions with tops, thinly
  sliced diagonally**

1 cup uncooked bulgur wheat

1 cup water

2 tablespoons lemon juice

**1 tablespoon chopped fresh
  mint leaves *or* ½ teaspoon
  dried mint**

Salt and black pepper

**Lemon peel and mint leaves
  (optional)**

1. Cut tomatoes in half crosswise. Scoop pulp and seeds out of tomatoes into medium bowl, leaving ¼-inch-thick shells.

2. Invert tomatoes on paper towel-lined plate; drain 20 minutes. Chop tomato pulp; set aside.

3. Heat oil in medium saucepan over medium-high heat. Cook and stir white parts of onions 1 to 2 minutes until wilted. Add bulgur; cook 3 to 5 minutes until browned.

4. Add reserved tomato pulp, water, lemon juice and mint to bulgur mixture. Bring to a boil over high heat; reduce heat to medium-low. Cover; simmer gently 15 to 20 minutes until liquid is absorbed.

5. Set aside a few sliced green onion tops for garnish; stir remaining green onions into bulgur mixture. Season with salt and pepper. Spoon mixture into tomato cups.*

6. Preheat oven to 400°F. Place filled cups in 13×9-inch baking dish; bake 15 minutes or until heated through. Top with reserved onion tops. Garnish with lemon peel and mint leaves. Serve immediately.

QUINOA-STUFFED EGGPLANT

Makes 2 servings

1 eggplant

¼ cup uncooked quinoa

½ cup water

2 teaspoons olive oil

½ cup chopped onion

1 clove garlic, chopped

2 cups baby spinach, finely
  chopped

¼ cup crumbled feta cheese,
  divided

Juice of 1 lemon

Chopped fresh parsley
  (optional)

1. Preheat oven to 400°F. Slice eggplant in half lengthwise. Scoop out flesh, leaving ½-inch shell. Finely chop scooped out flesh and set aside. Place eggplant halves in baking dish. Bake 30 minutes. *Reduce oven temperature to 350°F.*

2. Meanwhile, place quinoa in fine-mesh strainer; rinse well under cold running water. Bring water to a boil in small saucepan; stir in quinoa. Reduce heat to low; cover and simmer 10 to 15 minutes or until quinoa is tender and water is absorbed.

3. Heat oil in large skillet over medium-high heat. Add onion and chopped eggplant; cook and stir 10 minutes or until vegetables are browned and tender. Add garlic; cook and stir 1 minute. Remove from heat. Stir in quinoa, spinach, 2 tablespoons feta cheese and lemon juice.

4. Spoon quinoa mixture evenly into eggplant shells. Top evenly with remaining 2 tablespoons feta cheese.

5. Bake 15 minutes or until eggplant has softened and cheese is browned. Garnish with parsley.

ASIAN NOODLE SKILLET

Makes 4 servings

- **4 ounces soba (buckwheat) noodles**
- **2 tablespoons vegetable oil, divided**
- **1 pound firm tofu, cut into 1-inch cubes**
- **4 cloves garlic, minced**
- **1 tablespoon minced fresh ginger**
- **1 can (8 ounces) water chestnuts**
- **1 cup baby corn**
- **1½ cups mushroom or vegetable broth**
- **2 tablespoons soy sauce**
- **1 cup snow peas**
- **¼ cup green onions, thinly sliced**

1. Bring about 6 cups water to boil in large saucepan. Add noodles. Boil 1 minute or until wilted. Rinse under cold water and drain.

2. Heat 1 tablespoon oil in large nonstick skillet over medium-high heat. Add tofu. Brown tofu on all sides. Remove to plate. Add remaining 1 tablespoon oil to skillet. Add garlic and ginger. Cook and stir about 1 minute or until fragrant. Stir in water chestnuts and corn.

3. Return browned tofu to skillet. Add broth, soy sauce, snow peas and drained noodles. Bring to boil. Reduce heat; simmer 3 minutes or until noodles are cooked through and most of liquid has evaporated. Stir in green onions.

VEGGIE "MEATBALLS"

Makes 4 servings

½ **cup water**

¾ **cup bulgur wheat**

2 **teaspoons olive oil**

3 **medium portobello mushrooms (10 ounces), stemmed and diced**

1 **small onion, chopped**

1 **small zucchini (6 ounces), coarsely grated**

1 **teaspoon Italian seasoning**

2 **cloves garlic, minced**

¼ **cup sun-dried tomatoes (not packed in oil*), chopped**

4 **ounces grated Parmesan cheese**

2 **egg whites**

2 **cups marinara sauce, heated**

*If unavailable you may substitute ¼ cup sun-dried tomatoes packed in oil, well drained, patted dry and chopped.

1. Preheat oven to 375°F. Line large rimmed baking sheet with foil; spray with nonstick cooking spray.

2. Bring water to a boil in small saucepan; remove from heat. Stir in bulgur; cover and let stand while preparing vegetables.

3. Heat oil in large nonstick skillet over medium-high heat. Add mushrooms, onion, zucchini and Italian seasoning; cook and stir about 8 minutes or until softened. Add garlic; cook and stir 1 minute. Stir in tomatoes.

4. Transfer mushroom mixture to large bowl; let cool slightly. Add bulgur, Parmesan cheese and egg whites; mix well. Shape mixture into 12 balls using ¼ cup for each. Place meatballs on prepared baking sheet.

5. Bake 20 minutes. Turn meatballs; bake 8 to 10 minutes or until well browned. Serve hot with marinara sauce.

BARLEY AND SWISS CHARD SKILLET CASSEROLE

Makes 4 servings

- 1 cup water
- 1 cup chopped red bell pepper
- 1 cup chopped green bell pepper
- ¾ cup uncooked quick-cooking barley
- ⅛ teaspoon garlic powder
- ⅛ teaspoon red pepper flakes
- 2 cups packed coarsely chopped Swiss chard*
- 1 cup canned navy beans, rinsed and drained
- 1 cup quartered cherry tomatoes
- ¼ cup chopped fresh basil
- 1 tablespoon olive oil
- 2 tablespoons Italian-seasoned dry bread crumbs

Fresh spinach or beet greens can be substituted for Swiss chard.

1. Preheat broiler.

2. Bring water to a boil in large ovenproof skillet; add bell peppers, barley, garlic powder and red pepper flakes. Reduce heat; cover and simmer 10 minutes or until liquid is absorbed. Remove from heat.

3. Stir in chard, beans, tomatoes, basil and oil. Sprinkle with bread crumbs. Broil 2 minutes or until golden.

FARRO VEGGIE BURGERS

Makes 6 servings

1½ **cups water**

½ **cup pearled farro** *or* **spelt**

2 **medium potatoes, peeled and quartered**

2 **to 4 tablespoons canola oil, divided**

¾ **cup finely chopped green onions**

1 **cup grated carrots**

2 **teaspoons grated fresh ginger**

2 **tablespoons ground almonds**

¼ **to ¾ teaspoon salt**

¼ **teaspoon black pepper**

½ **cup panko bread crumbs**

6 **whole wheat hamburger buns**

Ketchup and mustard (optional)

1. Combine 1½ cups water and farro in medium saucepan; bring to a boil over high heat. Reduce heat to low; partially cover and cook 25 to 30 minutes or until farro is tender. Drain and cool. (If using spelt, use 2 cups of water and cook until tender.)

2. Meanwhile, place potatoes in large saucepan; cover with water. Bring to a boil; reduce heat and simmer 20 minutes or until tender. Cool and mash potatoes; set aside.

3. Heat 1 tablespoon oil in medium skillet over medium-high heat. Add green onions; cook and stir 1 minute. Add carrots and ginger; cover and cook 2 to 3 minutes or until carrots are tender. Transfer to large bowl; cool completely.

4. Add mashed potatoes and farro to carrot mixture. Add almonds, salt and pepper; mix well. Shape mixture into six patties. Spread panko on medium plate; coat patties with panko.

5. Heat 1 tablespoon oil in large nonstick skillet over medium heat. Cook patties about 4 minutes per side or until golden brown, adding additional oil as needed. Serve on buns with desired condiments.

Note: Farro is a whole grain and belongs to the wheat family. It's very close to spelt, and it is rich in fiber, magnesium and vitamins A, B, C and E. It has a nutty flavor and a chewy bite. It can be used in place of rice in many dishes.

SOBA STIR-FRY

Makes 4 servings

8 ounces uncooked soba (buckwheat) noodles

1 tablespoon olive oil

2 cups sliced shiitake mushrooms

1 medium red bell pepper, cut into thin strips

2 whole dried red chiles *or* ¼ teaspoon red pepper flakes

1 clove garlic, minced

2 cups shredded napa cabbage

½ cup vegetable broth

2 tablespoons tamari or soy sauce

1 tablespoon rice wine *or* dry sherry

2 teaspoons cornstarch

1 package (14 ounces) firm tofu, drained and cut into 1-inch cubes

2 green onions, thinly sliced

1. Cook noodles according to package directions, omitting salt. Drain and set aside.

2. Heat oil in large nonstick skillet or wok over medium-high heat. Add mushrooms, bell pepper, chiles and garlic. Cook and stir 3 minutes or until mushrooms are tender. Add cabbage. Cover; cook 2 minutes or until cabbage is wilted.

3. Whisk broth, tamari and rice wine into cornstarch in small bowl until smooth. Stir sauce into vegetable mixture. Cook 2 minutes or until sauce is thickened.

4. Stir in tofu and noodles; toss gently until heated through. Sprinkle with green onions. Serve immediately.

ITALIAN EGGPLANT WITH MILLET AND PEPPER STUFFING

Makes 4 servings

¼ **cup uncooked millet**

2 **small eggplants (about ¾ pound total)**

¼ **cup chopped red bell pepper, divided**

¼ **cup chopped green bell pepper, divided**

1 **teaspoon olive oil**

1 **clove garlic, minced**

1½ **cups vegetable broth**

½ **teaspoon ground cumin**

½ **teaspoon dried oregano**

⅛ **teaspoon red pepper flakes**

1. Cook and stir millet in large heavy skillet over medium heat 5 minutes or until golden. Transfer to small bowl; set aside.

2. Slice eggplants in half lengthwise. Scoop out flesh, leaving ¼-inch shell. Finely chop scooped out flesh; set aside. Combine 1 tablespoon red bell pepper and 1 tablespoon green bell pepper in small bowl; set aside.

3. Heat oil in same skillet over medium heat. Add chopped eggplant, remaining red and green bell pepper and garlic; cook and stir about 8 minutes or until eggplant is tender.

4. Stir in toasted millet, broth, cumin, oregano and red pepper flakes. Bring to a boil over high heat. Reduce heat to medium-low. Cook, covered, 35 minutes or until all liquid has been absorbed and millet is tender. Remove from heat; let stand, covered, 10 minutes.

5. Preheat oven to 350°F. Pour 1 cup water into 8-inch square baking pan. Fill eggplant shells with eggplant-millet mixture. Sprinkle with reserved chopped bell peppers, pressing in lightly. Carefully place filled shells in prepared pan. Bake 15 minutes or until heated through.

BOLIVIAN QUINOA HUMINTAS (TAMALES)

Makes 12 tamales

- **1 package (4 ounces) dried corn husks, *divided***
- **¼ cup (½ stick) butter**
- **1 medium onion, finely chopped**
- **2 cups cooked quinoa**
- **⅔ cup (5 fluid-ounce can) NESTLÉ® CARNATION® Evaporated Milk**
- **2 large eggs, lightly beaten**
- **1 tablespoon sugar**
- **1 teaspoon salt**
- **½ teaspoon anise seeds, crushed**
- **½ teaspoon ground cinnamon**
- **1 tablespoon hot yellow pepper paste or purée**
- **1 cup (4 ounces) shredded Chihuahua, mozzarella or Muenster cheese**
- **¼ cup grated Parmesan cheese (optional)**

SOAK 12 large or 24 small corn husks in warm water for at least 1 hour or until softened and easy to fold. (A plate placed on top of husks will help in keeping husks submerged.) Set aside *remaining* dry husks; they will be used later in recipe.

HEAT butter in small skillet over medium heat. Add onion; cook, stirring occasionally, for 3 minutes or until tender.

PLACE quinoa in a food processor; cover. Pulse a few times until coarsely ground. Add evaporated milk, cooked onion, quinoa, eggs, sugar, salt, anise, cinnamon, pepper paste and cheeses. Pulse until well blended. (The batter will be somewhat thick.)

PLACE one large or two small soaked corn husks overlapped on work surface. Spread ⅓ cup filling, using back of spoon, to form a square in the center of the lower half of husk(s). Fold left edge over filling. Fold pointy end of husk and tuck in while folding over right edge (one end will be open). Tie with strip of corn husk or twine. Repeat with *remaining* dry husks and filling.

PLACE vegetable steamer in large pot; add water to just below steamer. Arrange tamales upright in steamer rack. Cover top of tamales with *remaining* dry husks and a damp towel; cover with lid. Bring to a boil; reduce heat to low. Steam, adding water as needed, for about 30 to 45 minutes or until filling pulls away from the husks. Serve warm.

Prep Time: 1 hour

Cooking Time: 35 minutes

SWISS CHARD, BARLEY AND FETA GRATIN

Makes 8 servings

⅔ cup uncooked quick-cooking barley

12 cups (about 13 ounces) Swiss chard, ends trimmed and leaves and stems cut crosswise in ½-inch-wide strips

2 cups water

1 can (about 14 ounces) diced tomatoes, drained

¾ cup (3 ounces) crumbled feta cheese

½ teaspoon dried oregano

¼ teaspoon salt (optional)

⅛ teaspoon black pepper

1 tablespoon unsalted butter, melted

½ teaspoon garlic powder

⅔ cup fresh whole wheat bread crumbs*

½ cup vegetable broth

To make fresh bread crumbs, tear 1¼ slices bread into pieces; process in food processor until coarse crumbs form.

1. Preheat oven to 375°F. Spray 2-quart casserole with nonstick cooking spray.

2. Cook barley according to package directions, omitting any salt.

3. Place Swiss chard in large saucepan. Add water; cover and bring to a boil. Reduce heat and simmer 13 minutes or until tender. Drain.

4. Combine barley, Swiss chard, tomatoes, cheese, oregano, salt, if desired, and pepper in prepared casserole. Smooth into even layer.

5. Combine butter and garlic powder. Add bread crumbs; mix well. Pour broth over gratin; sprinkle evenly with crumb mixture.

6. Bake 20 minutes or until topping is golden brown. Let stand 5 minutes before serving.

Salads & Soups

QUINOA AND SHRIMP SALAD

Makes 4 to 6 servings

1 cup uncooked quinoa

2 cups water

½ teaspoon salt, divided

12 ounces thawed frozen cooked small shrimp, well drained

1 cup cherry or grape tomatoes, halved

¼ cup chopped fresh basil

2 tablespoons capers

2 tablespoons finely chopped green onion

3 tablespoons olive oil

1 to 2 tablespoons lemon juice

1 teaspoon grated lemon peel

⅛ teaspoon black pepper

1. Place quinoa in fine-mesh strainer. Rinse well under cold running water. Bring 2 cups water and ¼ teaspoon salt to a boil in medium saucepan over high heat. Stir in quinoa. Reduce heat to low; cover and simmer 10 to 15 minutes or until quinoa is tender and water is absorbed.

2. Combine quinoa, shrimp, tomatoes, basil, capers and green onion in large bowl. Whisk oil, lemon juice, lemon peel, pepper and remaining ¼ teaspoon salt in small bowl until well blended. Pour over salad; gently toss.

Tip: Soggy shrimp ruin the texture of this salad. To drain shrimp well, blot dry on paper towels.

BULGUR, TUNA, TOMATO AND AVOCADO SALAD

Makes 3 servings

⅔ cup water

⅓ cup uncooked bulgur

1 cup halved grape tomatoes

1 can (6 ounces) tuna packed in water, drained and flaked

¼ cup finely chopped red onion

1 large stalk celery, trimmed and thinly sliced

¼ cup finely chopped avocado

1 tablespoon minced fresh Italian parsley

1 to 2 tablespoons lemon juice

4 teaspoons chicken broth

1 teaspoon olive oil

⅛ teaspoon black pepper

1. Bring water to a boil in small saucepan. Stir in bulgur. Cover; reduce heat to low. Simmer 8 minutes or until bulgur swells and has absorbed most of the water. Remove from heat; cover and let stand 10 minutes.

2. Meanwhile, combine tomatoes, tuna, onion and celery in large bowl. Stir in bulgur, avocado and parsley. Combine lemon juice, broth, oil and pepper in small bowl. Pour over salad. Toss gently to mix. Chill 2 hours before serving.

Note: Bulgur wheat is wheat kernels that have been steamed, dried and crushed. Look for it in the rice and dried beans section or in the natural foods aisle of your supermarket.

BALSAMIC BERRY QUINOA SALAD

Makes 6 servings

2 cups water

1 cup quinoa

6 tablespoons WISH-BONE®
   Light Balsamic Basil
   Vinaigrette Dressing

1 large cucumber, seeded and
   chopped

1 cup strawberries, quartered,
   or raspberries

1 Granny Smith apple, peeled,
   cored and chopped

¼ cup finely chopped red onion,
   rinsed with cold water

1. Bring water to a boil over high heat in 2-quart saucepan. Stir in quinoa, then return to a boil. Reduce heat to medium and cook, covered, 12 minutes or until water is absorbed. Remove from heat, fluff, then let stand, covered, 15 minutes.

2. Combine hot quinoa with remaining ingredients in serving bowl. Chill, if desired.

Prep Time: 20 minutes

Cook Time: 12 minutes

Stand Time: 15 minutes

CHICKEN-BARLEY SOUP

Makes 6 servings

6 cups cold water

1½ pounds chicken thighs, skinned

2 stalks celery, sliced

2 carrots, thinly sliced

1 leek, sliced

1½ teaspoons salt

½ teaspoon dried marjoram leaves

¼ teaspoon black pepper

¼ teaspoon dried summer savory

1 herb bouquet*

⅓ cup quick-cooking barley

3 cups fresh spinach, chopped

¼ small red bell pepper, cut into matchsticks

Use any combination of herbs and spices, such as parsley stems, thyme sprigs, peppercorns, whole cloves, bay leaves and garlic cloves for herb bouquet. Wrap small bundle in cheesecloth and tie with string.

1. Combine water, chicken, celery, carrots, leek, salt, marjoram, black pepper, savory and herb bouquet in large saucepan Dutch oven; bring to a boil over high heat. Reduce heat to low; simmer, uncovered, 45 minutes or until chicken is tender.

2. Remove chicken to plate; let stand until cool enough to handle. Remove and discard herb bouquet. Skim foam and fat from soup with large spoon. (Or, refrigerate soup several hours and remove fat that rises to surface. Refrigerate chicken if chilling soup to remove fat.)

3. Add barley to soup; bring to a boil over high heat. Reduce heat to medium-low; simmer, uncovered, 10 minutes or until barley is almost tender. Meanwhile, remove chicken meat from bones; discard bones. Cut chicken into bite-size pieces.

4. Add chicken, spinach and bell pepper to soup; simmer 5 minutes or until spinach is wilted, bell pepper is tender and chicken is heated through. Season with additional salt and black pepper.

BARLEY AND CHICKEN SALAD

Makes 4 servings

⅔ **cup uncooked quick-cooking barley**

1½ **cups (about 6 ounces) coarsely chopped cooked boneless skinless chicken breast**

¾ **cup seedless red grapes, cut in half**

2 **tablespoons toasted chopped walnuts**

2 **tablespoons lemon juice**

1 **tablespoon orange juice**

1 **tablespoon extra-virgin olive oil**

¼ **teaspoon kosher salt**

⅛ **teaspoon black pepper**

3 **tablespoons finely chopped fresh Italian parsley**

1. Cook barley according to package directions omitting any salt or fat. Transfer to large bowl; cool to lukewarm.

2. Combine barley, chicken, grapes and walnuts in large bowl. Whisk together lemon juice, orange juice, oil, salt and pepper in small bowl. Pour over salad, sprinkle with parsley; toss gently.

ORANGE TWISTED QUINOA WALDORF SALAD

Makes 4 servings

½ **cup uncooked quinoa**

1 **cup water**

½ **cup quartered seedless grapes (green, purple and/or a combination)**

1 **small apple, chopped**

1 **stalk celery, chopped (about ⅓ cup)**

¼ **cup chopped walnuts, toasted**

¼ **cup plain nonfat Greek yogurt**

2 **tablespoons orange juice**

1½ **teaspoons honey**

¼ **teaspoon salt**

Dash black pepper

1 **cup canned mandarin oranges, drained**

Fresh mint leaves (optional)

1. Place quinoa in fine-mesh strainer; rinse well under cold running water. Bring water to a boil in small saucepan; stir in quinoa. Reduce heat to low; cover and simmer 10 to 15 minutes or until quinoa is tender and water is absorbed.

2. Place quinoa in large bowl. Stir in grapes, apple, celery and walnuts.

3. Whisk yogurt, orange juice, honey, salt and pepper in small bowl. Add to quinoa mixture; mix well. Add orange sections; toss gently. Garnish with mint.

GREENS, WHITE BEAN AND BARLEY SOUP

Makes 8 servings

2 tablespoons olive oil

3 carrots, diced

1½ cups chopped onions

2 cloves garlic, minced

1½ cups sliced mushrooms

6 cups vegetable broth

2 cups cooked barley

1 can (about 15 ounces)
  Great Northern beans,
  rinsed and drained

2 bay leaves

1 teaspoon sugar

1 teaspoon dried thyme

7 cups chopped stemmed
  collard greens (about
  24 ounces)

1 tablespoon white wine
  vinegar

  Hot pepper sauce

  Red bell pepper strips
  (optional)

1. Heat oil in Dutch oven over medium heat. Add carrots, onions and garlic; cook and stir 3 minutes. Add mushrooms; cook and stir 5 minutes or until carrots are tender.

2. Add broth, barley, beans, bay leaves, sugar and thyme. Bring to a boil over high heat. Reduce heat to medium-low; cover and simmer 5 minutes. Add greens; simmer 10 minutes. Remove and discard bay leaves. Stir in vinegar. Season with hot pepper sauce. Garnish with red bell peppers.

QUINOA & MANGO SALAD

Makes 8 servings

1 cup uncooked quinoa

2 cups water

2 cups cubed peeled mango
(about 2 large mangoes)

½ cup sliced green onions

½ cup dried cranberries

2 tablespoons chopped fresh
parsley

¼ cup extra virgin olive oil

1 tablespoon plus 1½ teaspoons
white wine vinegar

1 teaspoon Dijon mustard

½ teaspoon salt

⅛ teaspoon black pepper

1. Place quinoa in fine-mesh strainer; rinse well under cold running water. Combine quinoa and 2 cups water in medium saucepan; bring to a boil over high heat. Reduce heat to low; cover and simmer 10 to 12 minutes until quinoa is tender and water is absorbed. Stir quinoa; let stand, covered, 15 minutes. Transfer to large bowl; cover and refrigerate at least 1 hour.

2. Add mangoes, green onions, cranberries and parsley to quinoa; mix well.

3. Combine oil, vinegar, mustard, salt and pepper in small bowl; whisk until blended. Pour over quinoa mixture; mix until well blended.

Tip: This salad can be made several hours ahead and refrigerated. Allow it to stand at room temperature for at least 30 minutes before serving.

HEIRLOOM TOMATO QUINOA SALAD

Makes 4 servings

1 cup uncooked quinoa

2 cups water

2 tablespoons olive oil

1 tablespoon lemon juice

1 clove garlic, minced

½ teaspoon salt

2 cups assorted heirloom grape tomatoes (red, yellow and/ or a combination)

¼ cup crumbled feta cheese

¼ cup chopped fresh basil, plus additional basil leaves for garnish

1. Place quinoa in fine-mesh strainer; rinse well under cold running water. Bring 2 cups water to a boil in small saucepan; stir in quinoa. Reduce heat to low; cover and simmer 10 to 15 minutes or until quinoa is tender and water is absorbed.

2. Meanwhile, whisk oil, lemon juice, garlic and salt in large bowl until smooth and well blended. Gently stir in tomatoes and quinoa. Cover and refrigerate at least 30 minutes.

3. Stir in cheese just before serving. Top each serving with 1 tablespoon chopped basil. Garnish with additional basil leaves.

WHOLE WHEAT TACO SALAD BOWLS WITH MIXED GRAINS

Makes 4 servings

4 (8-inch) ORTEGA® Whole Wheat Flour Soft Tortillas

1 cup cooked quinoa

1 cup cooked barley

¼ cup B&G® Sliced Ripe Olives

¼ cup ORTEGA® Salsa, any variety

¼ cup fresh cilantro, chopped

1 tomato, diced

1 cup kale leaves, rinsed and thinly sliced

2 tablespoons olive oil

Salt and black pepper, to taste

PREHEAT oven to 350°F.

PLACE tortillas in 4-inch baking dish; bake 15 minutes until sides of tortillas curl and create bowls.

COMBINE quinoa, barley, olives, salsa, cilantro and tomato in medium bowl; mix well. Toss in kale and oil. Add salt and pepper to taste.

SERVE mixed grain salad in baked tortilla bowls.

Tip: Garnish with toasted pecans for an added crunch.

Prep: 10 minutes

Start to Finish: 30 minutes

BUTTERNUT SQUASH AND MILLET SOUP

Makes 6 servings

1 red bell pepper

1 teaspoon canola oil

2¼ cups diced butternut squash
    or 1 package (10 ounce)
    frozen diced butternut
    squash

1 medium red onion, chopped

1 teaspoon curry powder

½ teaspoon smoked paprika

½ teaspoon salt

⅛ teaspoon black pepper

2 cups chicken broth

2 boneless skinless chicken
    breasts (about 4 ounces
    each), cooked and chopped

1 cup cooked millet

1. Place bell pepper on rack in broiler pan 3 to 5 inches from heat source or hold over open gas flame on long-handled metal fork. Turn bell pepper often until blistered and charred on all sides. Transfer to resealable food storage bag; seal bag and let stand 15 to 20 minutes to loosen skin. Remove loosened skin with paring knife. Cut off top and scrape out seeds; discard.

2. Heat oil in large saucepan over high heat. Add squash, bell pepper and onion; cook and stir 5 minutes. Add curry powder, paprika, salt and black pepper. Pour in broth; bring to a boil. Cover and cook 7 to 10 minutes or until vegetables are tender.

3. Purée soup in saucepan with hand-held immersion blender or in batches in food processor or blender. Return soup to saucepan. Stir in chicken and millet; cook until heated through.

ZUPPA DE FARRO

Makes 6 servings

- 8 ounces whole cereal farro grain *or* quick pearl barley
- 4 ounces pancetta, chopped
- 1 small onion, sliced (about ¼ cup)
- 2 cloves garlic, minced
- 1 teaspoon dried thyme leaves, crushed
- 4 cups SWANSON® Chicken Broth (Regular, NATURAL GOODNESS® *or* Certified Organic)
- 2 medium plum tomatoes, chopped (about 1 cup)
- 1 tablespoon chopped fresh basil leaves
- ¼ teaspoon ground black pepper
- Parmesan cheese (optional)

1. Place the farro in a large bowl. Add water to cover and let soak for 1 hour. Drain. Place the farro in a 6-quart saucepot. Cover with 8 cups water. Heat to a boil. Cook for 30 minutes. Drain. Reserve farro.

2. In the same saucepot, cook the pancetta, onion, garlic and thyme over medium heat for about 10 minutes or until well browned. Add the broth and tomatoes. Heat to a boil. Reduce the heat to low. Cook for 10 minutes. Add the farro, basil and black pepper. Cook for 10 minutes more. Serve with cheese, if desired.

Kitchen Tip: If using quick pearl barley instead of farro, do not pre-cook. Add to the soup with the broth and tomatoes.

Prep Time: 1 hour 40 minutes

Cook Time: 35 minutes

ITALIAN QUINOA SALAD

Makes 4 servings

1⅓ cups water

⅔ cup uncooked quinoa

½ cup **WISH-BONE® Light Country Italian Dressing**

½ cup chopped mushrooms

½ cup chopped red bell pepper

½ cup chopped zucchini

¼ cup green onions, sliced

1 tablespoon chopped flat-leaf parsley

1. Bring water to a boil over high heat in 2-quart saucepan. Add quinoa and return to a boil. Reduce heat to medium and cook, covered, 12 minutes or until water is absorbed. Remove from heat, fluff and let stand covered 15 minutes.

2. Combine quinoa with remaining ingredients in serving bowl. Chill, if desired.

Note: Quinoa, a highly nutritious edible seed, is becoming more and more popular. Try it in this easy recipe.

Prep Time: 15 minutes

Cook Time: 12 minutes

Stand Time: 15 minutes

RIO STAR® GRAPEFRUIT & QUINOA SALAD

Makes 4 servings

1 Texas RIO STAR® Grapefruit, sectioned

8 thin slices fresh ginger

¼ cup extra-virgin olive oil

¾ cup quinoa

½ teaspoon kosher salt, plus additional for seasoning

1 tablespoon white wine vinegar

2 teaspoons honey

1 small serrano or jalapeño chile, minced (with seeds for maximum heat)

2 scallions (both white and green parts), minced

2 carrots, peeled and diced

2 tablespoons chopped fresh cilantro leaves

Freshly ground black pepper

1. Strip the peel from the grapefruit with a vegetable peeler, taking care not to include the bitter white pith. Warm the grapefruit peel, ginger and olive oil in a small saucepan over medium heat. As soon as the oil starts to bubble, after about 2 minutes, remove from heat. Set the oil aside to steep for 30 minutes. Strain and reserve the oil.

2. Meanwhile, rinse the quinoa in a bowl and drain. Put the quinoa in a small saucepan with 1½ cups water and ½ teaspoon salt. Boil over high heat, and then reduce heat to maintain a gentle simmer and cook, uncovered, for 15 minutes. Set aside off the heat, undisturbed, for 5 minutes. Transfer the quinoa to a bowl and fluff with a fork. Cool.

3. Segment the grapefruit over a bowl, reserving the segments and juice separately. Whisk 3 tablespoons of the grapefruit juice with the vinegar, honey and salt to taste in a medium bowl. Gradually whisk in 3 tablespoons of the reserved grapefruit oil, starting with a few drops and then adding the rest in a stream to make a slightly thick dressing. Season with pepper to taste.

4. Toss quinoa with the dressing, chile, scallions, carrots and cilantro. Season with salt and pepper, to taste.

5. Toss the grapefruit segments into the salad, divide among 4 plates. Serve warm or at room temperature.

Serving Suggestion: This salad is delicious served with grilled salmon.

Prep Time: 40 minutes

LENTIL-BARLEY SOUP

Makes 8 servings

6 cups water

1 can (28 ounces) diced
    tomatoes

¾ cup uncooked pearl barley

¾ cup dried lentils

½ cup chopped celery

¼ cup chopped onions

6 cubes vegetable bouillon

1 tablespoon fresh oregano *or*
    1 teaspoon dried oregano

1½ teaspoons fresh rosemary *or*
    ½ teaspoon dried rosemary

1 teaspoon lemon pepper

1 teaspoon minced garlic

1 cup thinly sliced carrots

1 cup shredded Swiss or
    mozzarella cheese

1. Combine water, tomatoes, barley, lentils, celery, onions, bouillon, oregano, rosemary, lemon pepper and garlic in large saucepan. Bring to a boil over high heat. Reduce heat; cover and simmer 45 minutes or until barley and lentils are tender, stirring occasionally.

2. Add carrots; simmer, covered, 15 minutes or until carrots are tender and soup is thickened. Sprinkle with cheese just before serving.

HEARTY MUSHROOM AND BARLEY SOUP

Makes 8 to 10 servings

9 cups chicken broth

1 package (16 ounces) sliced fresh mushrooms

1 onion, chopped

2 carrots, chopped

2 stalks celery, chopped

½ cup uncooked pearl barley

½ ounce dried porcini mushrooms

3 cloves garlic, minced

1 teaspoon salt

½ teaspoon dried thyme

½ teaspoon black pepper

Slow Cooker Directions

Combine broth, sliced mushrooms, onion, carrots, celery, barley, porcini mushrooms, garlic, salt, thyme and pepper in 5-quart slow cooker. Cover; cook on LOW 4 to 6 hours.

Variation: For even more flavor, add a beef or ham bone to the slow cooker with the rest of the ingredients.

Cook Time: 4 to 6 hours

BULGUR SALAD NIÇOISE

Makes 3 to 4 servings

2 cups water

¼ teaspoon salt

1 cup bulgur wheat

1 cup halved cherry tomatoes

1 can (6 ounces) tuna packed in
water, drained and flaked

½ cup pitted black niçoise
olives*

3 tablespoons finely chopped
green onions, green part
only

1 tablespoon chopped fresh
mint leaves (optional)

1½ tablespoons lemon juice, or to
taste

1 tablespoon olive oil

⅛ teaspoon black pepper

Mint leaves (optional)

If you use larger olives, slice or chop as desired.

1. Bring water and salt to a boil in medium saucepan. Stir in bulgur. Remove from heat. Cover and set aside 10 to 15 minutes or until water is absorbed and bulgur is tender. Fluff with fork; set aside to cool completely.

2. Combine bulgur, tomatoes, tuna, olives, green onions and chopped mint, if desired, in large bowl. Combine lemon juice, oil and pepper in small bowl. Pour over salad. Toss gently to mix well. Garnish with mint leaves, if desired.

BULGUR SALAD

Makes 6 servings

1¼ **cups water**

1 **cup uncooked bulgur wheat**

1 **cup PACE® Pico De Gallo *or* PACE® Picante Sauce**

1 **cup rinsed, drained canned black beans**

1 **cup drained canned whole kernel corn**

¼ **cup chopped fresh cilantro leaves**

1. Heat the water in a 2-quart saucepan over medium-high heat to a boil. Stir the bulgur into the saucepan. Remove the saucepan from the heat. Let stand for 20 minutes.

2. Stir the bulgur, pico de gallo, beans, corn and cilantro in a medium bowl. Serve immediately or cover and refrigerate until ready to serve.

Kitchen Tip: For a twist, stir in a squeeze of fresh lime juice.

Prep Time: 10 minutes

Cook Time: 5 minutes

Stand Time: 20 minutes

CALIFORNIA PLUM AND QUINOA SALAD

Makes 6 servings

1¼ cups quinoa

2½ cups boiling water

2 large ripe California plums, pitted and diced

½ cup chopped, toasted walnuts

¼ cup chopped red pepper

¼ cup chopped yellow bell pepper

¼ cup sliced green onion

3 tablespoons flax oil

3 tablespoons extra virgin olive oil

¼ cup white wine vinegar

1½ tablespoons honey

¼ teaspoon salt

Rinse quinoa and drain well. Add to boiling water; reduce heat and simmer, covered, for 12 minutes. Remove from heat and let stand for 5 minutes. Fluff with a fork and let chill for about 30 minutes. Stir together quinoa, plums, walnuts, peppers and onions in a medium bowl. Whisk together remaining ingredients in a small bowl and pour over salad; toss well to coat all ingredients with dressing. Cover and chill for 1 hour.

Prep Time: 20 minutes

Cook Time: 12-15 minutes

Chill Time: 1 hour

courtesy of
California Tree Fruit Agreement

TABBOULEH-STYLE AMARANTH SALAD

Makes 5 to 6 servings

2½ cups water

¾ cup dried amaranth*

2 cups chopped fresh parsley

8 ounces grape tomatoes, quartered

½ cup diced red onion

3 tablespoons capers, drained (optional)

4 medium cloves garlic, minced

1 ounce (¼ cup) pine nuts, toasted

2 tablespoons cider vinegar or red wine vinegar

1 tablespoon extra virgin olive oil

⅛ teaspoon red pepper flakes (optional)

¼ teaspoon salt

4 ounces (¾ cup) feta cheese, crumbled

Amaranth is an ancient whole grain and is very high in protein and fiber. In addition, it's gluten-free and a good source of iron and vitamin C. You can find it at the supermarket with the other grains or in bulk bins at health food stores.

1. Combine water and amaranth in large saucepan and bring to a boil over high heat. Reduce heat, cover and simmer 20 minutes or until most of the water is absorbed. (It will have a very soft consistency.)

2. Meanwhile, combine remaining ingredients except feta cheese in medium bowl; set aside.

3. Place amaranth in fine-mesh strainer; rinse well under cold running water until completely cooled. Shake off excess liquid, add to parsley mixture and toss until well blended. Stir in feta and toss gently.

Tip: It's important that the amaranth is placed in a fine-mesh strainer. The grain is so tiny and will slip through a traditional strainer. Strain in 2 or 3 batches if using a small-mesh strainer.

SHRIMP AND SOBA NOODLE SALAD

Makes 4 servings

4 ounces soba noodles*

2 cups diagonally sliced green beans (bite-size pieces)

1½ cups sliced mushrooms

1½ cups (6 ounces) cooked medium shrimp (with tails on)

¼ cup thinly sliced red bell pepper

2 tablespoons orange juice

2 tablespoons lime juice

1 tablespoon soy sauce

2 teaspoons dark sesame oil

2 tablespoons finely chopped fresh cilantro

1 to 2 tablespoons toasted sesame seeds (optional)

Soba is a Japanese noodle made from buckwheat flour with a different taste and texture from the kind of spaghetti most familiar to Americans. You can find them in Asian markets. If unavailable, you may substitute with linguine.

1. Cook noodles according to package directions omitting any salt or fat. Drain, rinse under warm water. Drain again and transfer to large bowl.

2. Coat large skillet with nonstick cooking spray; heat over medium-high heat. Add green beans and mushrooms; cook, mixing occasionally, 8 minutes or until mushrooms are lightly browned and beans are softened.

3. Combine noodles, shrimp, green bean mixture and bell pepper. In small bowl, whisk orange juice, lime juice, soy sauce and sesame oil. Pour over salad, sprinkle with cilantro and sesame seeds, if desired. Toss gently.

MEDITERRANEAN BARLEY SALAD

Makes 4 servings

1⅓ cups water

⅔ cup quick-cooking barley

½ cup diced roasted red peppers

12 pitted kalamata olives, coarsely chopped

12 turkey pepperoni slices, halved

¼ cup chopped red onion

2 ounces crumbled feta cheese

1 teaspoon dried basil

¼ teaspoon red pepper flakes

1 can (16 ounces) navy beans

1 can (14 ounces) sliced hearts of palm, drained

1 tablespoon extra virgin olive oil

1 tablespoon cider vinegar

Salt and black pepper (optional)

1. Bring water to a boil in medium saucepan over high heat. Add barley; return to a boil. Reduce heat; cover and simmer 15 minutes or until barley is tender.

2. Meanwhile, combine roasted peppers, olives, pepperoni, onion, cheese, basil and red pepper flakes in medium bowl.

3. Place barley and beans in colander; run under cold water until barley is cool and beans are rinsed. Add barley, beans, hearts of palm, oil, vinegar, salt and pepper to roasted pepper mixture; toss gently. Cover tightly and refrigerate until ready to serve.

BULGUR, GREEN BEAN & ORANGE SALAD

Makes 6 servings

⅔ cup bulgur

⅔ cup boiling water

1½ cups green beans, cut into 1-inch pieces

2 tablespoons olive oil

2 tablespoons lemon juice

½ teaspoon Greek seasoning

¼ teaspoon salt

¼ teaspoon black pepper

1 can (11 ounces) mandarin orange sections, drained

¼ cup slivered red onion

Spinach leaves (optional)

1. Place bulgur in medium bowl. Pour boiling water over bulgur; stir. Cover with plastic wrap; let stand 20 minutes or until bulgur is tender.

2. Meanwhile, cook beans in boiling water in small saucepan 6 to 7 minutes or until tender; drain.

3. To prepare dressing, combine oil, lemon juice, Greek seasoning, salt and pepper in small bowl; whisk until well blended. Set aside.

4. Add beans, orange sections and onion to bulgur. Drizzle dressing over salad; toss gently until well blended. Cover and refrigerate at least 30 minutes. Serve on spinach leaves, if desired.

On the Side

QUINOA-STUFFED TOMATOES

Makes 8 servings

½ **cup uncooked quinoa**

1 **cup water**

½ **teaspoon salt, divided**

1 **tablespoon olive oil**

1 **red bell pepper, chopped**

⅓ **cup chopped green onions**

⅛ **teaspoon black pepper**

⅛ **teaspoon dried thyme**

1 **tablespoon butter**

8 **plum tomatoes,* halved lengthwise, seeded, hollowed out**

*Or, substitute 4 medium tomatoes.

1. Preheat oven to 325°F. Place quinoa in fine-mesh strainer; rinse well under cold running water. Bring 1 cup water and ¼ teaspoon salt to a boil in small saucepan; stir in quinoa. Cover and reduce heat to low; simmer 12 to 14 minutes or until quinoa is tender and water is absorbed.

2. Heat oil in large skillet over medium-high heat. Add bell pepper; cook and stir 7 to 10 minutes or until tender. Stir in quinoa, green onions, remaining ¼ teaspoon salt, black pepper and thyme. Add butter; stir until melted. Remove from heat.

3. Arrange tomato halves in 13×9-inch baking dish. Fill with quinoa mixture.

4. Bake 15 to 20 minutes or until tomatoes are tender.

BARLEY "CAVIAR"

Makes 8 servings

4 cups water

½ teaspoon salt, divided

¾ cup uncooked pearl barley

½ cup sliced pimiento-stuffed olives

½ cup finely chopped red bell pepper

1 stalk celery, chopped

1 large shallot, finely chopped

1 jalapeño pepper,* minced, *or* ¼ teaspoon red pepper flakes

2 tablespoons plus 1 teaspoon olive oil

4 teaspoons white wine vinegar

¼ teaspoon ground cumin

⅛ teaspoon black pepper

8 leaves endive or Bibb lettuce

Jalapeño peppers can sting and irritate the skin, so wear rubber gloves when handling peppers and do not touch your eyes.

1. Bring water and ¼ teaspoon salt to a boil in medium saucepan over high heat. Stir in barley. Reduce heat to low; cover and simmer 45 minutes or until barley is tender. Remove from heat; let stand 5 minutes. Rinse under cold water; drain well. Place in large bowl.

2. Stir in olives, bell pepper, celery, shallot and jalapeño. Stir together oil, vinegar, remaining ¼ teaspoon salt, cumin and black pepper in small bowl. Pour over barley mixture; stir gently to mix well. Let stand 10 minutes. To serve, spoon barley mixture evenly into endive leaves.

CHILE AND LIME QUINOA

Makes 4 servings

½ **cup uncooked quinoa**

1 **cup water**

1 **small jalapeño pepper,***
    minced

2 **tablespoons finely chopped**
    green onion

2 **tablespoons olive oil**

1 **tablespoon fresh lime juice**

¼ **teaspoon salt**

¼ **teaspoon ground cumin**

¼ **teaspoon chili powder**

⅛ **teaspoon black pepper**

*Jalapeño peppers can sting and irritate the skin, so wear rubber gloves when handling peppers and do not touch your eyes.

1. Place quinoa in fine-mesh strainer; rinse well under cold running water.

2. Combine quinoa and water in small saucepan; bring to a boil over high heat. Reduce heat to low; cover and simmer 12 to 15 minutes or until quinoa is tender and water is absorbed. Cover; let stand 5 minutes.

3. Stir jalapeño pepper, green onion, oil, lime juice, salt, cumin, chili powder and black pepper into quinoa. Fluff mixture with fork. Serve warm or at room temperature.

WILD MUSHROOM QUINOA STUFFING

Makes 6 servings

1 cup uncooked quinoa

2 tablespoons olive oil, divided

2 cups vegetable broth

1 teaspoon poultry seasoning

½ teaspoon salt

1 small onion, diced

8 ounces cremini mushrooms, sliced

8 ounces shiitake mushrooms, stemmed and sliced

½ cup diced celery

2 tablespoons chopped fresh parsley (optional)

1. Place quinoa in fine-mesh strainer; rinse well under cold running water.

2. Heat 1 tablespoon oil in medium saucepan over medium-high heat. Add quinoa; stir until evenly coated. Stir in broth, poultry seasoning and salt. Bring to a boil. Reduce heat to low; cover and simmer 15 to 20 minutes or until quinoa is tender and broth is absorbed. Remove from heat.

3. Meanwhile, heat remaining 1 tablespoon oil in large skillet over medium heat. Add onion, mushrooms and celery; cook and stir 8 to 10 minutes or until vegetables are tender.

4. Combine quinoa and vegetables in large bowl. Sprinkle with parsley, if desired.

Turkey Stuffing: For extra flavor or for a festive meal, follow the recipe directions for the quinoa and spoon inside a turkey and roast according to recipe directions.

BARLEY & VEGETABLE RISOTTO

Makes 6 servings

2 teaspoons olive oil

1 small onion, diced

8 ounces sliced mushrooms

¾ cup uncooked pearl barley

1 large red bell pepper, diced

4 ½ cups vegetable or chicken broth

2 cups packed baby spinach

¼ cup grated Parmesan cheese

¼ teaspoon black pepper

Slow Cooker Directions

1. Heat olive oil in large nonstick skillet over medium-high heat. Add onion, cook and stir until lightly browned, about 2 minutes. Add mushrooms; cook 5 minutes, stirring frequently or until mushrooms begin to brown. Transfer to slow cooker.

2. Add barley, bell pepper, and broth. Cover; cook on LOW 4 to 5 hours or on HIGH 2½ to 3 hours, or until barley is tender and liquid is absorbed. Stir in spinach. Let stand 5 minutes. Gently stir in Parmesan cheese and black pepper just before serving.

MILLET PILAF

Makes 6 servings

1 tablespoon olive oil

½ onion, finely chopped

½ red bell pepper, finely chopped

1 carrot, finely chopped

2 cloves garlic, minced

1 cup uncooked millet

3 cups water

Grated peel and juice of 1 lemon

¾ teaspoon salt

¼ teaspoon black pepper

2 tablespoons chopped fresh parsley (optional)

1. Heat oil in medium saucepan over medium heat. Add onion, bell pepper, carrot and garlic; cook and stir 5 minutes or until softened. Add millet; cook and stir 5 minutes or until lightly toasted.

2. Stir in water, lemon peel, lemon juice, salt and black pepper; bring to a boil. Reduce heat to low; cover and simmer 30 minutes or until water is absorbed and millet is tender. Cover and let stand 5 minutes. Fluff with fork. Sprinkle with parsley, if desired.

QUINOA & ROASTED VEGETABLES

Makes 6 servings

2 medium sweet potatoes, cut into ½-inch-thick slices

1 medium eggplant, peeled and cut into ½-inch cubes

1 medium tomato, cut into wedges

1 large green bell pepper, sliced

1 small onion, cut into wedges

½ teaspoon salt

¼ teaspoon black pepper

¼ teaspoon ground red pepper

1 cup uncooked quinoa

2 cloves garlic, minced

½ teaspoon dried thyme

¼ teaspoon dried marjoram

2 cups water *or* vegetable broth

1. Preheat oven to 450°F. Line large jelly-roll pan with foil; spray with nonstick cooking spray.

2. Arrange sweet potatoes, eggplant, tomato, bell pepper and onion on prepared pan; spray lightly with cooking spray. Sprinkle with salt, black pepper and ground red pepper; toss to coat. Roast 20 to 30 minutes or until vegetables are browned and tender.

3. Meanwhile, place quinoa in fine-mesh strainer; rinse well under cold running water. Spray medium saucepan with cooking spray; heat over medium heat. Add garlic, thyme and marjoram; cook and stir 1 to 2 minutes. Add quinoa; cook and stir 2 to 3 minutes. Stir in water; bring to a boil over high heat. Reduce heat to low. Simmer, covered, 15 to 20 minutes or until water is absorbed. (Quinoa will appear somewhat translucent.) Transfer quinoa to large bowl; gently stir in roasted vegetables.

FRUIT & NUT QUINOA

Makes 6 servings

1 cup uncooked quinoa

2 cups water

2 tablespoons finely grated
  orange peel, plus additional
  for garnish

¼ cup fresh orange juice

2 teaspoons olive oil

½ teaspoon salt

¼ teaspoon ground cinnamon

⅓ cup dried cranberries

⅓ cup toasted pistachio nuts*

*To toast pistachios, spread in single layer in heavy
skillet. Cook over medium heat 1 to 2 minutes or
until nuts are lightly browned, stirring frequently.*

1. Place quinoa in fine-mesh strainer; rinse well under cold running water. Bring 2 cups water to a boil in small saucepan; stir in quinoa. Reduce heat to low; cover and simmer 10 to 15 minutes or until quinoa is tender and water is absorbed. Stir in 2 tablespoons orange peel.

2. Whisk orange juice, oil, salt and cinnamon in small bowl. Pour over quinoa; gently toss to coat. Fold in cranberries and pistachios. Serve warm or at room temperature. Garnish with additional orange peel.

BULGUR PILAF WITH TOMATO AND ZUCCHINI

Makes 8 servings

1 cup uncooked bulgur wheat

1 tablespoon olive oil

¾ cup chopped onion

2 cloves garlic, minced

1 can (about 14 ounces) whole tomatoes, drained and coarsely chopped

½ pound zucchini (2 small), thinly sliced

1 cup vegetable broth

1 teaspoon dried basil

⅛ teaspoon black pepper

1. Rinse bulgur thoroughly under cold water, removing any debris. Drain well; set aside.

2. Heat oil in large saucepan over medium heat. Add onion and garlic; cook and stir 3 minutes or until onion is tender. Stir in tomatoes and zucchini; reduce heat to medium-low. Cook, covered, 15 minutes or until zucchini is almost tender, stirring occasionally.

3. Stir bulgur, broth, basil and pepper into vegetable mixture. Bring to a boil over high heat. Cover; remove from heat. Let stand, covered, 10 minutes or until liquid is absorbed. Stir gently before serving.

QUINOA AND ROASTED CORN

Makes 6 to 8 servings

1 cup uncooked quinoa

2 cups water

½ teaspoon salt

4 ears corn *or* 2 cups frozen corn

¼ cup plus 1 tablespoon vegetable oil, divided

1 cup chopped green onions, divided

1 teaspoon coarse salt

1 cup quartered grape tomatoes or chopped plum tomatoes, drained*

1 cup black beans, rinsed and drained

Juice of 1 lime (about 2 tablespoons)

¼ teaspoon grated lime peel

¼ teaspoon sugar

¼ teaspoon ground cumin

¼ teaspoon black pepper

*Place tomatoes in fine-mesh strainer and place over bowl 10 to 15 minutes.

1. Place quinoa in fine-mesh strainer; rinse well under cold running water. Combine quinoa, water and salt in medium saucepan; bring to a boil over high heat. Reduce heat to low; cover and simmer 15 to 18 minutes or until quinoa is tender and water is absorbed. Transfer to large bowl.

2. Meanwhile, remove husks and silk from corn; cut kernels off cobs. Heat ¼ cup oil in large skillet over medium-high heat. Add corn; cook 10 to 12 minutes or until tender and lightly browned, stirring occasionally. Stir in ⅔ cup green onions and coarse salt; cook and stir 2 minutes. Add corn mixture to quinoa. Gently stir in tomatoes and black beans.

3. Combine lime juice, lime peel, sugar, cumin and pepper in small bowl. Whisk in remaining 1 tablespoon oil until blended. Pour over quinoa mixture; toss lightly to coat. Sprinkle with remaining ⅓ cup green onions. Serve warm or chilled.

BULGUR WITH ASPARAGUS AND SPRING HERBS

Makes 4 servings

⅔ **cup uncooked bulgur**

2 **cups sliced asparagus (1-inch pieces)**

½ **cup frozen peas, thawed**

⅔ **cup chopped fresh Italian parsley**

2 **teaspoons finely chopped fresh mint**

3 **tablespoons lemon juice**

1 **tablespoon orange juice**

1 **tablespoon extra virgin olive oil**

⅛ **teaspoon salt**

⅛ **teaspoon black pepper**

1. Prepare bulgur according to package directions, omitting any salt or fat. Drain well.

2. Steam asparagus in steamer basket over boiling water 3 to 4 minutes or until bright green and crisp-tender. Cool under cold running water, drain well; blot with paper towels.

3. Combine bulgur, asparagus, peas, parsley and mint in large bowl. Whisk lemon juice, orange juice, oil, salt and pepper in small bowl. Pour over bulgur mixture; toss gently.

Note: Bulgur is a whole grain that's high in fiber and protein. It's also a good source of iron, magnesium, and B vitamins.

QUINOA WITH TOMATO, BROCCOLI AND FETA

Makes 4 servings

⅔ cup uncooked quinoa

1½ cups small broccoli florets

1 plum tomato, cut into small cubes

⅓ cup (1½ ounces) crumbled feta cheese

2 tablespoons lemon juice

1 tablespoon extra virgin olive oil

¼ teaspoon dried dill weed or dried basil

¼ teaspoon kosher salt (optional)

⅛ teaspoon black pepper

1. Cook quinoa according to package directions omitting any salt or fat. Transfer to large bowl; cool to lukewarm.

2. Steam broccoli in steamer basket over boiling water 3 minutes or until just tender.

3. Combine quinoa, broccoli, tomato and feta.

4. In small bowl, whisk lemon juice, oil, dill weed, salt, if desired, and pepper. Pour over salad; toss gently.

SPICY SESAME NOODLES

Makes 6 servings

**6 ounces uncooked soba
(buckwheat) noodles**

2 teaspoons dark sesame oil

1 tablespoon sesame seeds

½ cup chicken broth

**1 tablespoon creamy peanut
butter**

½ cup thinly sliced green onions

½ cup minced red bell pepper

4 teaspoons soy sauce

**1½ teaspoons finely chopped
seeded jalapeño pepper***

1 clove garlic, minced

¼ teaspoon red pepper flakes

**Jalapeño peppers can sting and irritate the skin, so
wear rubber gloves when handling peppers and do
not touch your eyes.*

1. Cook noodles according to package directions. (Do not overcook.) Rinse noodles thoroughly with cold water; drain. Place noodles in large bowl; toss with oil.

2. Cook sesame seeds in small skillet over medium heat about 3 minutes or until seeds begin to pop and turn golden brown, stirring frequently. Remove from skillet.

3. Whisk broth and peanut butter in medium bowl until blended. (Mixture may look curdled.) Stir in green onions, bell pepper, soy sauce, jalapeño pepper, garlic and red pepper flakes.

4. Pour mixture over noodles; toss to coat. Cover and let stand 30 minutes at room temperature or refrigerate up to 24 hours. Sprinkle with toasted sesame seeds before serving.

BARLEY, HAZELNUT AND PEAR STUFFING

Makes 6 to 8 servings

3 to 3¼ cups vegetable broth, divided

½ teaspoon salt, divided

1 cup uncooked pearl barley

2 tablespoons butter, divided

1 small onion, chopped

1 stalk celery, chopped

1 large ripe pear,* unpeeled, cut into ½-inch dice

⅛ teaspoon black pepper

½ cup chopped toasted hazelnuts

Anjou pear is preferred.

1. Bring 3 cups broth and ¼ teaspoon salt to a boil in large saucepan over high heat. Stir in barley. Reduce heat to low. Simmer 45 minutes or until barley is tender. Remove from heat; set aside.

2. Melt 1 tablespoon butter in large skillet over medium heat. Add onion and celery. Cook and stir 5 minutes. Add remaining 1 tablespoon butter. Stir in pear. Cook and stir 5 minutes. Add barley, remaining ¼ teaspoon salt and pepper. If mixture is dry, add remaining ¼ cup broth. Stir in hazelnuts.

Serving Suggestion: Spoon stuffing mixture into baked acorn or butternut squash halves. Place stuffed squash in preheated 325°F oven; bake 15 to 20 minutes or until heated through.

Tip: To toast hazelnuts, preheat oven to 325°F. Spread hazelnuts on baking sheet; bake 5 to 7 minutes. Place nuts in a kitchen towel and rub to remove skins. Coarsely chop as needed.

LOW-CARB TABBOULEH

Makes 6 servings

¼ **cup fine-grain bulgur wheat**

¼ **cup water**

1 **tablespoon lemon juice**

¼ **cup extra virgin olive oil**

1½ **cups peeled, seeded and diced cucumbers**

1 **cup chopped flat-leaf (Italian) parsley**

1½ **cups diced tomatoes (3 medium tomatoes)**

¼ **cup chopped green onions**

¼ **cup freshly chopped mint leaves**

2 **teaspoons finely chopped walnuts**

1 **teaspoon chopped garlic**

Salt to taste

1. Place bulgur in medium bowl; add water and let sit 30 minutes or until all liquid is absorbed. Stir in lemon juice and oil.

2. Combine cucumbers, parsley, tomatoes, green onions, mint, walnuts and garlic. Add to barley. Season with salt.

3. Chill at least 2 hours, stirring occasionally.

BARLEY WITH CURRANTS AND PINE NUTS

Makes 4 servings

1 tablespoon butter

1 onion, finely chopped

2 cups chicken or vegetable broth

½ cup uncooked pearl barley

½ teaspoon salt

¼ teaspoon black pepper

⅓ cup currants

¼ cup pine nuts

Slow Cooker Directions

1. Melt butter in small skillet over medium-high heat. Add onion; cook 5 minutes or until lightly browned, stirring occasionally. Transfer to slow cooker. Add broth, barley, salt and pepper. Stir in currants. Cover; cook on LOW 3 hours.

2. Stir in pine nuts; serve immediately.

BULGUR PILAF WITH CARAMELIZED ONIONS & KALE

Makes 6 servings

1 tablespoon olive oil

**1 small onion, cut into thin
wedges**

1 clove garlic, minced

2 cups chopped kale

**2 cups vegetable or chicken
broth**

¾ cup medium grain bulgur

½ teaspoon salt

¼ teaspoon black pepper

1. Heat oil in large nonstick skillet over medium heat until hot. Add onion; cook about 8 minutes, stirring frequently or until softened and lightly browned. Add garlic; cook and stir 1 minute. Add kale; cook and stir about 1 minute or until kale is wilted.

2. Stir in broth, bulgur, salt and pepper. Bring to a boil. Reduce and simmer 12 minutes, covered or until liquid is absorbed and bulgur is tender.

BUCKWHEAT BROWNS

Makes 6 servings

1 cup cooked soba noodles, drained and chopped well

⅓ cup bacon, crisp-cooked and crumbled

⅓ cup minced fresh parsley

¼ cup minced red bell pepper

1 teaspoon minced garlic

1 egg white, beaten until foamy

½ teaspoon black pepper

1. Combine noodles, bacon, parsley, bell pepper, garlic and egg white in medium bowl; stir well. Add black pepper; stir. (Egg white will be partially absorbed.)

2. Spray large skillet with nonstick cooking spray; heat over medium-high heat. Use ¼ cup measure to scoop noodle mixture onto skillet. Cook 3 to 4 minutes. Spray each noodle cluster with cooking spray; turn and cook 3 to 4 minutes or until noodles are browned at edges. Serve warm.

SPINACH-PINE NUT WHOLE GRAIN PILAF

Makes 6 servings

2 cups hot cooked brown rice or bulgur

1½ ounces pine nuts *or* slivered almonds, toasted

2 ounces spinach leaves, coarsely chopped

1 tablespoon extra virgin olive oil

1 teaspoon dried basil leaves

½ teaspoon salt

¼ teaspoon red pepper flakes

Place hot rice in large bowl. Add pine nuts, spinach, oil, basil, salt and red pepper flakes. Toss gently, yet thoroughly until spinach is slightly wilted.

WILD RICE CASSEROLE

Makes 6 servings

1 cup wild rice, soaked
    overnight, drained

1 large onion, chopped

1 cup (4 ounces) shredded
    Cheddar cheese

1 cup chopped mushrooms

1 cup chopped black olives

1 cup drained chopped
    tomatoes

1 cup tomato juice

⅓ cup vegetable oil

    Salt and black pepper

1. Preheat oven to 350°F.

2. Combine rice, onion, cheese, mushrooms, olives, tomatoes, tomato juice and oil in large bowl. Transfer rice mixture to 2½- to 3-quart casserole. Season with salt and pepper.

3. Cover and bake 1½ hours or until rice is tender.

Snacks & Sweets

WHOLE GRAIN CHIPPERS

Makes about 6 dozen cookies

1 cup butter, softened

1 cup packed light brown sugar

⅔ cup granulated sugar

2 eggs

1 teaspoon baking soda

1 teaspoon vanilla

   Pinch salt

2 cups old-fashioned oats

1 cup all-purpose flour

1 cup whole wheat flour

1 package (12 ounces)
   semisweet chocolate chips

1 cup sunflower seeds

1. Preheat oven to 375°F. Lightly grease cookie sheets or line with parchment paper.

2. Beat butter, sugars and eggs in large bowl with electric mixer until light and fluffy. Beat in baking soda, vanilla and salt. Blend in oats and flours to make stiff dough. Stir in chocolate chips. Shape rounded teaspoonfuls of dough into balls; roll in sunflower seeds. Place 2 inches apart on prepared cookie sheets.

3. Bake 8 to 10 minutes or until firm. Do not overbake. Cool 2 minutes on cookie sheets; remove to wire racks to cool completely.

WHOLE-GRAIN BANANA BREAD

Makes 8 to 10 servings

¼ cup plus 2 tablespoons wheat germ, divided

⅔ cup butter, softened

1 cup sugar

2 eggs

1 cup mashed bananas (2 to 3 bananas)

1 teaspoon vanilla

1 cup all-purpose flour

1 cup whole wheat pastry flour

1 teaspoon baking soda

½ teaspoon salt

½ cup chopped walnuts or pecans (optional)

Slow Cooker Directions

1. Spray 1-quart casserole, soufflé dish or other high-sided baking pan with nonstick cooking spray. Sprinkle dish with 2 tablespoons wheat germ.

2. Beat butter and sugar in large bowl on medium speed of electric mixer until fluffy. Add eggs, one at a time; beat until blended. Add bananas and vanilla; beat until smooth.

3. Gradually stir in flours, remaining ¼ cup wheat germ, baking soda and salt. Stir in nuts, if desired. Pour batter into prepared dish; place in slow cooker. Cover; cook on HIGH 2 to 3 hours or until edges begin to brown and toothpick inserted into center comes out clean.

4. Remove dish from slow cooker. Cool on wire rack about 10 minutes. Remove bread from dish; cool completely on wire rack.

WHOLE GRAIN BANANA FRUIT 'N' NUT BARS

Makes 24 bars

1¼ cups whole wheat flour

2 teaspoons pumpkin pie spice

½ teaspoon baking soda

¼ teaspoon salt

½ cup (1 stick) light butter

⅔ cup firmly packed brown sugar

1 large egg

1¼ cups mashed ripe bananas (about 3 small bananas)

1½ cups QUAKER® Oats (quick or old fashioned, uncooked)

⅔ cup chopped pitted dates or golden raisins

⅔ cup chopped toasted walnuts

1. Heat oven to 350°F. Lightly spray 13×9×2-inch metal baking pan with nonstick cooking spray. Stir together flour, pumpkin pie spice, baking soda and salt in medium bowl; mix well. Set aside.

2. Beat butter and brown sugar in large bowl with electric mixer until well blended. Add egg and bananas; mix well. (Mixture will look curdled.) Add flour mixture; beat on low just until well blended. Stir in oats, dates and walnuts. Spread evenly in prepared pan.

3. Bake 20 to 25 minutes, until edges are golden brown and wooden pick inserted in center comes out with a few moist crumbs clinging to it. Cool completely in pan on wire rack. Cut into bars.

Note: To store, wrap tightly in foil and store up to 2 days at room temperature. For longer storage, label and freeze in airtight container up to 3 months. Defrost, uncovered, at room temperature.

Cook's tip: To toast nuts, spread in single layer on cookie sheet. Bake at 350°F about 6 to 8 minutes or until lightly browned and fragrant, stirring occasionally. Cool before using. Or, spread in single layer on microwave-safe plate. Microwave on HIGH (100% power) 1 minute; stir. Continue to microwave on HIGH, checking every 30 seconds, until nuts are fragrant and brown. Cool before using.

NO-BAKE FRUIT AND GRAIN BARS

Makes 16 bars

½ **cup cooked amaranth**

2 **cups whole grain puffed rice cereal**

½ **cup chopped dried fruit**

½ **cup honey**

¼ **cup sugar**

¾ **cup almond butter**

*Amaranth can be found in health food stores in the bulk bins. It may also be found in large supermarkets in the health food aisle.

1. Spray 8- or 9-inch square baking pan with nonstick cooking spray.

2. Heat medium saucepan over high heat. Add 1 tablespoon amaranth; stir or gently shake saucepan until almost all seeds have popped. (Partially cover saucepan if seeds are popping over the side.) Remove to medium bowl. Repeat with remaining amaranth.

3. Stir cereal and dried fruit into popped amaranth.

4. Combine honey and sugar in same saucepan; bring to a boil over medium heat. Remove from heat; stir in almond butter until melted and smooth.

5. Pour honey mixture over cereal mixture; stir until evenly coated. Press firmly into prepared pan. Let stand until set. Cut into bars.

Note: Amaranth is a gluten-free whole grain that's high in protein and fiber. Cooked amaranth is tender with a slight crunch. It doesn't fluff up like rice, but instead has a dense quality that retains moisture.

WHOLE GRAIN CRANBERRY CHOCOLATE CHIP COOKIES

Makes about 18 cookies

1½ **cups five-grain cereal, uncooked**

1 **cup whole wheat flour**

½ **teaspoon salt**

½ **teaspoon baking soda**

¼ **teaspoon baking powder**

½ **cup (1 stick) unsalted butter, softened**

⅓ **cup packed brown sugar**

1 **egg**

½ **teaspoon vanilla**

½ **cup golden raisins**

½ **cup semisweet chocolate chips**

½ **cup sweetened dried cranberries, chopped**

1. Preheat oven to 350°F. Spray nonstick cookie sheet with nonstick cooking spray. Combine cereal, flour, salt, baking soda and baking powder in medium bowl.

2. Beat butter and brown sugar in large bowl with electric mixer at medium speed until light and fluffy. Beat in egg and vanilla until well blended. Beat in flour mixture just until blended. Fold in raisins, chocolate chips and cranberries. Drop dough by tablespoonfuls 2 inches apart onto prepared cookie sheet.

3. Bake in center of oven 7 to 9 minutes or until golden. Transfer cookies to wire rack to cool completely.

Variations: Substitute other multigrain cooked cereals for the five-grain cereal. For additional flavor variations, you can also experiment with other dried fruit, such as dried apricots or cherries. Just be sure to chop the fruit well to evenly distribute it among the cookies.

WHOLE GRAIN QUACKERS

½ **cup plus 2 tablespoons old-fashioned oats**

½ **cup whole wheat flour**

½ **teaspoon salt**

4 **tablespoons cold butter, cut into chunks**

¼ **cup milk**

2 **tablespoons honey**

Sea salt or cinnamon sugar (optional)

1. Preheat oven to 375°F. Place oats in bowl of food processor; pulse until coarse flour forms.

2. Add whole wheat flour and salt; pulse to combine. Add butter; pulse until pea-size pieces form. Heat milk with honey in small microwavable measuring cup on high 45 seconds or until honey dissolves.

3. Add milk mixture through feed tube of processor with motor running. When ball of dough forms on top of blade (less than 2 minutes), remove to lightly floured surface.

4. Roll dough with floured rolling pin very thin. Lightly flour cookie sheet. Cut small duck or other shapes with cookie cutters and transfer to cookie sheet. Sprinkle with sea salt or cinnamon sugar, if desired.

5. Bake on middle rack 6 to 10 minutes or until quackers are slightly browned. Watch carefully. Some quackers may brown more quickly. Remove finished quackers from cookie sheet and return other to oven if necessary. Remove to wire rack to cool.

GLUTEN FREE GRAHAM CRACKERS

Makes about 12 crackers

½ **cup sweet rice flour (mochiko),* plus additional for work surface**

½ **cup sorghum flour**

½ **cup packed brown sugar**

⅓ **cup tapioca flour**

½ **teaspoon baking soda**

½ **teaspoon salt**

¼ **cup (½ stick) margarine or dairy-free margarine**

2 **tablespoons plus 2 teaspoons whole milk or dairy-free milk**

2 **tablespoons honey**

1 **tablespoon vanilla**

*Sweet rice flour is usually labeled mochiko (the Japanese term). It is available in the Asian section of large supermarkets, at Asian grocers and on the Internet.

1. Combine ½ cup sweet rice flour, sorghum flour, brown sugar, tapioca flour, baking soda and salt in food processor; pulse to combine, making sure brown sugar is free of lumps. Add margarine; pulse until coarse crumbs form.

2. Whisk milk, honey and vanilla in small bowl or measuring cup until well blended and honey is dissolved. Pour into flour mixture; process until dough forms. (Dough will be very soft and sticky.)

3. Transfer dough to floured surface; pat into rectangle. Wrap in plastic wrap and refrigerate at least 4 hours or up to 2 days.

4. Preheat oven to 325°F. Cover work surface with parchment paper; generously dust with sweet rice flour.

5. Roll dough to ⅛-inch-thick rectangle on parchment paper using rice-floured rolling pin. (If dough becomes too sticky, return to refrigerator or freezer for several minutes.) Place dough on parchment paper on baking sheet. Score dough into cracker shapes (do not cut all the way through). Prick dough in rows with tines of fork. Place baking sheet in freezer 5 to 10 minutes or in refrigerator 15 to 20 minutes.

6. Bake chilled crackers 25 minutes or until firm and slightly darkened. Transfer parchment to wire rack to cool. Cut crackers when cooled slightly.

Serving Suggestion: Serve crackers as a snack or for s'mores with chocolate and marshmallows.

POWER-PACKED SNACK BARS

Makes 16 bars

3 cups puffed millet cereal

1 cup dried fruit bits

¼ cup roasted unsalted sunflower kernels

1 teaspoon ground cinnamon

½ cup creamy soynut butter

½ cup honey

2 tablespoons packed brown sugar

1. Line 8- to 9-inch square baking pan with parchment paper. Spray with nonstick cooking spray.

2. Combine millet, dried fruit, sunflower kernels and cinnamon in large bowl; mix well.

3. Combine soynut butter, honey and brown sugar in small microwavable bowl. Microwave on HIGH 15 seconds or until melted and smooth.

4. Stir soynut butter mixture into millet mixture until well combined and evenly coated. Press firm into prepared pan. Cover and refrigerate at least 2 hours or until firm. To serve, cut into bars.

FRUITED GRANOLA

Makes about 20 servings

3 cups quick oats

1 cup sliced almonds

1 cup honey

½ cup wheat germ or honey
    wheat germ

3 tablespoons butter or
    margarine, melted

1 teaspoon ground cinnamon

3 cups whole grain cereal flakes

½ cup dried blueberries or
    golden raisins

½ cup dried cranberries or
    cherries

½ cup dried banana chips or
    chopped pitted dates

1. Preheat oven to 325°F.

2. Spread oats and almonds in single layer in 13×9-inch baking pan. Bake 15 minutes or until lightly toasted, stirring frequently.

3. Combine honey, wheat germ, butter and cinnamon in large bowl until well blended. Add oats and almonds; toss to coat completely. Spread mixture in single layer in baking pan. Bake 20 minutes or until golden brown. Cool completely in pan on wire rack. Break mixture into chunks.

4. Combine oat chunks, cereal, blueberries, cranberries and banana chips in large bowl. Store in airtight container at room temperature up to 2 weeks.

Tip: Prepare this granola on the weekend and you'll have a scrumptious snack or breakfast treat on hand for the rest of the week!

KIWI GREEN DREAM

Makes 2 servings

¾ **cup water**

2 **kiwis, peeled and quartered**

½ **cup frozen pineapple chunks**

½ **avocado, pitted and peeled**

1 **tablespoon chia seeds**

1. Combine water, kiwis, pineapple and avocado in blender; blend until smooth.

2. Add chia seeds; blend until smooth. Serve immediately.

CHERRY BERRY POMEGRANATE SMOOTHIE

Makes 2 servings

¾ **cup water**

1 **cup frozen dark sweet cherries**

½ **cup frozen strawberries**

½ **cup pomegranate seeds**

1 **teaspoon lemon juice**

1 **tablespoon chia seeds**

1. Combine water, cherries, strawberries, pomegranate seeds and lemon juice in blender; blend until smooth.

2. Add chia seeds; blend until smooth. Serve immediately.

ACKNOWLEDGMENTS

The publisher would like to thank the companies and organizations listed below
for the use of their recipes and photographs in this publication.

The Beef Checkoff
California Tree Fruit Agreement
Campbell Soup Company
National Onion Association
Nestlé USA
Ortega®, A Division of B&G Foods North America, Inc.
Pinnacle Foods
TexaSweet Citrus Marketing, Inc.
The Quaker® Oatmeal Kitchens
Washington Apple Commission

METRIC CONVERSION CHART

VOLUME MEASUREMENTS (dry)

1/8 teaspoon = 0.5 mL
1/4 teaspoon = 1 mL
1/2 teaspoon = 2 mL
3/4 teaspoon = 4 mL
1 teaspoon = 5 mL
1 tablespoon = 15 mL
2 tablespoons = 30 mL
1/4 cup = 60 mL
1/3 cup = 75 mL
1/2 cup = 125 mL
2/3 cup = 150 mL
3/4 cup = 175 mL
1 cup = 250 mL
2 cups = 1 pint = 500 mL
3 cups = 750 mL
4 cups = 1 quart = 1 L

VOLUME MEASUREMENTS (fluid)

1 fluid ounce (2 tablespoons) = 30 mL
4 fluid ounces (1/2 cup) = 125 mL
8 fluid ounces (1 cup) = 250 mL
12 fluid ounces (1 1/2 cups) = 375 mL
16 fluid ounces (2 cups) = 500 mL

WEIGHTS (mass)

1/2 ounce = 15 g
1 ounce = 30 g
3 ounces = 90 g
4 ounces = 120 g
8 ounces = 225 g
10 ounces = 285 g
12 ounces = 360 g
16 ounces = 1 pound = 450 g

DIMENSIONS

1/16 inch = 2 mm
1/8 inch = 3 mm
1/4 inch = 6 mm
1/2 inch = 1.5 cm
3/4 inch = 2 cm
1 inch = 2.5 cm

OVEN TEMPERATURES

250°F = 120°C
275°F = 140°C
300°F = 150°C
325°F = 160°C
350°F = 180°C
375°F = 190°C
400°F = 200°C
425°F = 220°C
450°F = 230°C

BAKING PAN SIZES

Utensil	Size in Inches/Quarts	Metric Volume	Size in Centimeters
Baking or	8×8×2	2 L	20×20×5
Cake Pan	9×9×2	2.5 L	23×23×5
(square or	12×8×2	3 L	30×20×5
rectangular)	13×9×2	3.5 L	33×23×5
Loaf Pan	8×4×3	1.5 L	20×10×7
	9×5×3	2 L	23×13×7
Round Layer	8×1½	1.2 L	20×4
Cake Pan	9×1½	1.5 L	23×4
Pie Plate	8×1¼	750 mL	20×3
	9×1¼	1 L	23×3
Baking Dish	1 quart	1 L	—
or Casserole	1½ quart	1.5 L	—
	2 quart	2 L	—